DIGITAL
UTILITY BELT

TREY CARMICHAEL
STEPHEN SWANSON

TABLE OF CONTENTS

INTRODUCTION

It was a dark and stormy night in Gotham City. The streets were slick with rain, reflecting the neon lights and the ever-present sense of danger in the air. The Joker, Batman's notorious arch-nemesis, had once again concocted a diabolical scheme to bring chaos to the city. But little did he know, the caped crusader was ready for action, his trusty utility belt by his side.

You might be thinking, "What does Batman have to do with my business software?" Well, dear reader, the answer is simple: just like the Dark Knight relies on his utility belt, every business owner needs a digital utility belt to navigate the perilous world of modern technology. The right combination of software tools can make or break a business, but figuring out which ones to use can feel like a cluster f*ck. That's where we come in.

Picture this: Batman, dangling precariously over a vat of toxic waste, with the Joker cackling maniacally in the background. To the untrained eye, it might seem like the end for our hero. But Batman knows that his utility belt holds the keys to his survival. With a quick flick of his wrist, he deploys a grappling hook, swings to safety, and ultimately foils the Joker's evil plan.

In the business world, your digital utility belt is your arsenal of software tools that help you tackle various tasks, streamline processes, and ultimately save the day. But unlike Batman, who has Alfred to guide him through the seemingly endless array of gadgets, you may not have a trusty sidekick to help you navigate the chaos of software selection. That's where the "Digital Utility Belt" comes in.

The software landscape is vast and ever-changing, making it challenging to keep up with the latest innovations and decide which tools are worth your time and investment. It can feel like a never-ending journey through a technological menagerie, where one wrong turn can leave you lost and confused. That's why we, Trey Carmichael and

Stephen Swanson, have joined forces to become your Alfred and Lucius Fox.

In the pages of this book, you'll find a comprehensive guide to the tools and software that can help you conquer the chaos and make your business thrive. We'll introduce you to tools for project management, communication, automation, and more. We'll also explore how to choose the right software for your unique needs, how to integrate these tools into your workflow, and how to evaluate their effectiveness.

So strap on your metaphorical cape and cowl, dear reader, for we are about to embark on a thrilling adventure through the world of digital utility belts. Together, we'll explore the vast technological landscape, armed with the knowledge and guidance to help you become the superhero your business needs. Remember, the night is darkest just before the dawn, and we promise to be the light that guides you through the chaos.

Stay tuned, true believers, for in the upcoming chapters, you'll learn how to build your very own digital utility belt perfectly tailored to your business's unique challenges and goals. With the right tools and know-how, you'll be able to conquer any obstacle, defeat any villain, and rise to greatness.

DOMAIN NAMES

In today's digital landscape, your online presence can be the difference between success and failure, personally and professionally. Your domain name is a critical component of that presence. It serves as your digital address, a unique identifier that sets you apart in the vast expanse of the internet. In this chapter, we'll delve into the importance of domain names, guide you through choosing a domain registrar, and outline the process of securing your domain name. We'll also discuss which domain names you should obtain to bolster your digital identity.

Section 1.1: The Importance of Domain Names

A domain name is more than just a web address; it's the foundation of your online brand. It represents your online identity and is often your first impression on potential customers, partners, or employers. A strong domain name can help establish credibility, build trust, and drive engagement with your online content. Therefore, choosing and securing the right domain name is crucial to your success in the digital realm.

Section 1.2: Choosing a Domain Registrar

When choosing a domain registrar, there's no one-size-fits-all solution. Instead, each provider offers a unique set of features, pricing structures, and levels of customer support. To help you navigate this landscape, we'll discuss five popular domain registrars: GoDaddy, Domain.com, Namecheap, Google Domains, and Network Solutions.

GoDaddy: As one of the largest domain registrars, GoDaddy offers a vast selection of domain extensions and competitive prices. Their platform includes an easy-to-use domain management interface and 24/7 customer support. However, GoDaddy has been criticized for aggressive upselling tactics and cluttered user interfaces.

Domain.com: Known for its simplicity and ease of use, Domain.com offers a wide range of domain extensions and additional services, such as hosting and website-building tools. Their pricing is competitive, but they may charge extra for certain features like WHOIS privacy.

Namecheap: Namecheap offers affordable pricing and a user-friendly platform. They provide free WHOIS privacy protection, which can be a significant advantage for those looking to keep their personal information private. Namecheap also offers a wide range of services, such as hosting and SSL certificates.

Google Domains: Google Domains is a newer player in the domain registrar market. They offer a clean and straightforward interface, competitive pricing, and free WHOIS privacy protection. In addition, as a Google product, it can be easily integrated with other Google services, making it a convenient choice for those already invested in the Google ecosystem.

Network Solutions: As one of the oldest domain registrars, Network Solutions has a long history in the industry. They offer a wide range of domain extensions, but their pricing can be higher than competitors. Network Solutions also provides additional services such as hosting, email, and website-building tools.

Section 1.3: Securing Your Domain Name

Once you've chosen a domain registrar, follow these steps to secure your domain name:

Brainstorm: Consider the purpose of your website and your target audience. Then, generate a list of potential domain names that are memorable, easy to spell, and reflective of your brand or personal identity.

Research: Check the availability of your desired domain names using the domain search tool provided by your chosen registrar. If your preferred domain name is unavailable, consider alternative domain extensions or slight variations in spelling.

Register: Once you've found an available domain name, register through your domain registrar. This typically involves providing your contact information, selecting the registration term, and submitting payment.

Protect your privacy: If your registrar offers WHOIS privacy protection, consider opting for this service. WHOIS privacy protection helps keep your personal information, such as your name, phone number, and address, hidden from the public WHOIS database. This can reduce the risk of spam, identity theft, and unwanted contact.

Set up domain renewal reminders: Domain names are registered for a specific period, usually between one and ten years. To avoid losing your domain name due to expiration, set up reminders for the renewal date or opt for automatic renewal if your registrar offers it.

Section 1.4: Choosing the Right Domain Names for Your Needs

When selecting domain names, there are several factors to consider. You'll want to consider your brand, business name, or core product offerings. Here are some tips to help you choose the right domain names for your needs:

Personal Name: If you're building a personal brand or portfolio, consider registering your full name as a domain name. This can help establish your online presence and make it easy for potential clients or employers to find you.

Business Name: Securing a domain name that matches your company name is essential for businesses. This ensures consistency across all your branding efforts and helps customers find you online.

Core Product Names: If your business offers a specific product or service, consider registering a domain name that reflects your core offering. This can help attract targeted traffic and improve search engine rankings for relevant keywords.

Alternative Extensions: It's not uncommon for popular domain names to be taken in the .com extension. If your desired domain name is unavailable, consider alternative extensions such as .net, .org, .co, or even industry-specific extensions like .tech or .design.

Defensive Registrations: To protect your brand from cybersquatting or potential confusion, consider registering multiple domain names, including common misspellings, variations, or alternative extensions. This can help ensure your target audience finds you, even if they mistyped your domain name.

Section 1.5: Conclusion

Your domain name is the foundation of your digital identity. Therefore, it's essential to carefully consider your options, choose a reliable domain registrar, and secure the right domain names for your personal or business needs. By following the guidance provided in this chapter, you'll be well on your way to establishing a robust online presence and reaping the benefits of a well-chosen domain name. Remember, your domain name is more than just an address—it's the key to unlocking your digital kingdom.

WEB BUILDERS

Having secured the perfect domain name, it's time to create a website representing your personal or business brand. This chapter will explore web builders, their role in website creation, and how to choose between popular options such as Go High Level, WordPress, Wix, and Google Sites. We'll also guide getting started with each platform to help you establish your digital home.

Section 2.1: What is a Web Builder?

A web builder, also known as a website builder or site builder, is a tool or platform that simplifies website creation. These builders often feature drag-and-drop functionality, allowing users to design and customize their websites without requiring extensive coding knowledge. Web builders are an excellent option for individuals and businesses looking to create a professional online presence with minimal time investment and technical expertise.

Section 2.2: Choosing a Web Builder

When selecting a web builder, it's essential to consider your specific needs, budget, and level of technical proficiency. This section will compare four popular web builders: Go High Level, WordPress, Wix, and Google Sites.

Go High Level: Go High Level is an all-in-one marketing platform for digital agencies and small businesses. It offers a robust web builder and a suite of marketing tools such as CRM, email marketing, and sales funnel creation. This platform is well-suited for businesses looking to streamline their marketing efforts and quickly build a professional website. However, it may be more expensive and feature-rich than an individual or small business owner needs.

WordPress: WordPress is one of the most popular web builders, powering approximately 40% of all websites globally. It offers a versatile platform with thousands of themes and plugins, making it highly customizable. While WordPress has a steeper learning curve than other builders, it's flexibility and extensive user community make it an attractive option for those looking to create a unique, scalable website.

Wix: Wix is a user-friendly web builder that offers a wide range of templates and an intuitive drag-and-drop editor. It's an excellent option for individuals and small businesses looking to create a visually appealing website without coding expertise. However, Wix may be less suitable for more complex sites or those requiring advanced customization.

Google Sites: Google Sites is a free, straightforward web builder allowing users to create simple websites quickly. It's ideal for those seeking a temporary or essential online presence with minimal investment. However, its limited features and customization options make it less suitable for professional or more sophisticated websites.

Section 2.3: Getting Started with Your Chosen Web Builder

Once you've chosen a web builder, it's time to start creating your website. Below, we'll outline the initial steps for each platform.

Go High Level: To begin, sign up for a Go High-Level account and select a subscription plan that best suits your needs. Next, connect your domain name and choose a website template. Next, customize the template using the drag-and-drop editor, add your content, and integrate any additional marketing tools as needed. Finally, publish your website to make it live.

WordPress: Start by choosing a hosting provider that supports WordPress, such as Bluehost or SiteGround. Install WordPress on your hosting account, connect your domain name, and select a theme for your website. Customize your site using the built-in editor or install plugins for additional functionality. Add your content, and once you're satisfied, publish your website.

Wix: Sign up for a Wix account and choose a subscription plan based on your needs. Select a template, customize it using the drag-and-drop editor, and connect your domain name. Next, add your content, including text, images, and multimedia elements. You can also integrate additional features, such as contact forms or e-commerce functionality, through the Wix App Market. Once satisfied with your site, click "Publish" to make it live.

Google Sites: To get started with Google Sites, log in to your Google account, and navigate to the Google Sites homepage. Click "Create" to start a new site, and choose a template or start from scratch. Customize your site using the drag-and-drop editor, and add your content. Connect your domain name or use a subdomain provided by Google. Once your site is complete, click "Publish" to make it live.

Section 2.4: Tips for Building an Effective Website

Regardless of the web builder you choose, there are several best practices to remember when creating your website. These tips will help you create a professional and engaging online presence:

Keep your design clean and uncluttered: A simple, organized layout makes it easier for visitors to navigate your site and find the information they're seeking.

Optimize for mobile devices: With more users accessing websites on their smartphones and tablets, ensuring your site is responsive and easy to use on various screen sizes is essential.

Prioritize user experience: Focus on creating a seamless experience for your visitors by ensuring quick load times, clear calls to action, and easy-to-use navigation.

Use high-quality visuals: Incorporate professional images, graphics, or videos to enhance your site's visual appeal and support your written content.

Optimize for search engines: Use relevant keywords, create unique content, and include meta tags and descriptions to help improve your site's search engine rankings.

Regularly update your content: Keep your site fresh and relevant by adding new content, updating existing information, and removing outdated material.

Monitor and analyze your site's performance: Use analytics tools to track visitor behavior, identify areas for improvement, and make data-driven decisions to enhance your site's effectiveness.

Section 2.5: Conclusion

Selecting the right web builder is crucial to creating a successful online presence. By considering your specific needs, budget, and technical proficiency, you can choose a platform that aligns with your goals. Once you've selected a web builder, follow the steps outlined in this chapter to get started on your website creation journey. Remember to keep best practices in mind, focusing on user experience, mobile optimization, and search engine visibility. With dedication and the right tools, you'll be well on your way to crafting a digital home that reflects your personal or business brand and attracts visitors worldwide.

WEB HOSTING

If you've decided to build your website using WordPress, selecting a web hosting provider is one of your most critical decisions. In this chapter, we'll discuss the importance of web hosting, compare popular providers such as Amazon AWS, SiteGround, Bluehost, Ionos, and GreenGeeks, and guide you through getting started with each.

Section 3.1: The Importance of Web Hosting

Web hosting is the service that provides the necessary resources for your website to be accessible on the internet. Your hosting provider stores your website files on servers and makes them available to users when requested. Your website's performance, security, and reliability depend heavily on your chosen hosting provider. Therefore, selecting the right web host is crucial to your website's success.

Section 3.2: Comparing Web Hosting Providers for WordPress

This section will examine five popular web hosting providers that support WordPress, discussing their features, pricing, and advantages.

Amazon AWS: Amazon Web Services (AWS) is a cloud-based hosting solution known for its scalability, flexibility, and performance. AWS offers various services, including its Elastic Compute Cloud (EC2) and Lightsail, which can be used for hosting WordPress websites. AWS is well-suited for businesses with variable traffic or those looking to scale rapidly. However, its pricing model can be complex, and managing AWS requires some technical expertise.

SiteGround: SiteGround is a popular hosting provider that offers managed WordPress hosting plans, including automatic updates, daily backups, and free SSL certificates. SiteGround is known for its reliable performance, excellent customer support, and focus on security. Their pricing is competitive, but higher-traffic websites may require more expensive plans.

Bluehost: Bluehost is a user-friendly hosting provider that offers affordable WordPress hosting plans. They provide easy WordPress installation, a free domain name, and a custom control panel for managing your website. Bluehost's performance and customer support are generally well-regarded, making them popular for beginners and small businesses.

Ionos: Ionos, formerly known as 1&1, offers a range of hosting plans tailored to WordPress users. They provide managed WordPress hosting with automatic updates, daily backups, and free SSL certificates. Ionos is known for its scalable solutions and affordable pricing, but customer support reviews can be mixed.

GreenGeeks: GreenGeeks is an eco-friendly hosting provider that focuses on sustainable practices, offsetting their energy usage with renewable energy credits. They offer managed WordPress hosting with automatic updates, free SSL certificates, and daily backups. GreenGeeks' performance and customer support are highly regarded, and their commitment to sustainability sets them apart from competitors.

Section 3.3: Tips for Choosing the Right Web Hosting Provider

When selecting a web hosting provider for your WordPress site, consider the following factors:

Compatibility: Ensure the hosting provider is compatible with the latest version of WordPress and meets its minimum requirements, such as PHP and MySQL versions.

Performance: Look for hosting providers with a track record of reliable performance, fast load times, and minimal downtime.

Customer support: Choose a hosting provider that offers responsive, knowledgeable customer support to assist you with any technical issues that may arise.

Scalability: Select a hosting provider that can accommodate your website's growth, with plans that offer increased resources and bandwidth as needed.

Security: Opt for hosting providers that prioritize security, offering features such as SSL certificates, automated backups, and malware scanning.

Pricing: Compare hosting plans and pricing to find a provider that offers the features you need at a price you can afford. Be sure to consider any additional costs, such as domain registration, SSL certificates, or premium plugins.

Section 3.4: Getting Started with Your Chosen Web Hosting Provider

Once you've selected a web hosting provider that best suits your needs, follow these steps to set up your WordPress website:

Sign up for a hosting plan: Choose a hosting plan that aligns with your requirements, such as the number of websites, storage, and bandwidth. Complete the registration process and make the necessary payment.

Register or connect your domain name: If you don't already have a domain name, register one with your hosting provider or a separate domain registrar. If you have a domain name, update the DNS settings to point to your hosting provider's nameservers.

Install WordPress: With most hosting providers, installing WordPress is a simple process. Follow the provider's instructions to install WordPress, usually through a one-click installation or a custom control panel.

Configure your website: Login to your WordPress dashboard, where you can choose a theme, install plugins, and customize your site. Then, add your content, such as pages, blog posts, images, and multimedia elements.

Set up security and performance enhancements: To keep your website secure and running smoothly, consider installing security plugins, setting up a caching solution, and optimizing images for faster load times.

Test your website: Before launching your website, test it on multiple devices and browsers to ensure it functions correctly and displays as intended.

Launch your website: Once you're satisfied with your site, make it live by updating your domain's DNS settings (if necessary) and announcing the launch to your audience.

Section 3.5: Conclusion

Choosing the right web hosting provider is a crucial step in creating a successful WordPress website. By considering factors such as compatibility, performance, customer support, scalability, security, and pricing, you can select a provider that meets your needs and ensures your website's success. Once you've chosen a provider, follow the steps outlined in this chapter to set up your WordPress site, configure it to your liking, and launch it for the world to see. With a solid foundation in place, you'll be well on your way to building a thriving online presence.

E-COMMERCE STORE BUILDERS

As the world of e-commerce continues to grow, choosing the right platform for your online store is critical. In this chapter, we'll explore e-commerce store builders, discuss their role in creating digital storefronts, and provide guidance on selecting the right one for your business. We'll also provide an overview of popular options such as Shift4Shop, Shopify, Ecwid, and WooCommerce for WordPress.

Section 4.1: What is an E-commerce Store Builder?

An e-commerce store builder is a software or platform designed to help businesses create, manage, and scale their online stores. These builders simplify the process of setting up an e-commerce website by providing templates, tools, and integrations that make it easy to add and manage products, process payments, and handle shipping and taxes. By choosing the right e-commerce store builder, you can create a user-friendly and efficient online shopping experience for your customers.

Section 4.2: Choosing an E-commerce Store Builder for Your Business

When selecting an e-commerce store builder, consider factors such as your technical expertise, the size and complexity of your product catalog, your budget, and your desired level of customization. Additionally, pay attention to each platform's available integrations, ease of use, and scalability to ensure it meets your business's unique needs.

Section 4.3: Overview of Popular E-commerce Store Builders

In this section, we'll provide an overview of four popular e-commerce store builders: Shift4Shop, Shopify, Ecwid, and WooCommerce for WordPress.

Shift4Shop: Shift4Shop (formerly 3dcart) is a comprehensive e-commerce platform that offers a wide range of features and customization options. It includes built-in SEO tools, a robust set of shipping and payment integrations, and a variety of design templates. Shift4Shop is a good fit for businesses of all sizes, but its interface may have a steeper learning curve for those with limited technical expertise.

Shopify: Shopify is a popular, user-friendly e-commerce platform suitable for businesses of all sizes. It offers a variety of customizable themes, a large app store for added functionality, and built-in payment processing through Shopify Payments. Shopify's pricing plans accommodate various budgets, making it an attractive option for startups and established businesses alike.

Ecwid: Ecwid is a versatile e-commerce platform that can be integrated with existing websites, social media platforms, and marketplaces. Its ease of use, seamless integrations, and flexible pricing make it an excellent choice for small businesses looking to add e-commerce functionality to their existing online presence. However, Ecwid may not be the best fit for larger businesses or those looking for a standalone e-commerce solution.

WooCommerce: WooCommerce is a powerful, open-source e-commerce plugin for WordPress websites. It offers extensive customization options, a large library of plugins and themes, and seamless integration with the WordPress ecosystem. WooCommerce is well-suited for businesses with an existing WordPress site or those looking for a flexible, scalable e-commerce solution. However, it may require more technical expertise than other platforms.

Section 4.4: Getting Started with Your Chosen E-commerce Store Builder

Once you've selected an e-commerce store builder that aligns with your business needs, follow these steps to set up your online store:

Sign up for an account: Register for an account with your chosen e-commerce platform, and select a pricing plan that meets your requirements.

Choose a theme or template: Select a design template that aligns with your brand and offers a user-friendly shopping experience.

Customize your store: Use the platform's customization tools to tailor your store's design, layout, and functionality to your specific needs.

Add your products: Upload your product information, including descriptions, images, pricing, and inventory levels. Organize your products into categories to make it easier for customers to browse your store.

Set up payment and shipping options: Choose your preferred payment gateway, and configure shipping options and rates based on your business's needs.

Ensure that you have SSL encryption enabled to protect your customers' payment information.

Configure tax settings: Set up tax rules for your store based on your location and any applicable regulations.

Test your store: Before launching your store, thoroughly test its functionality, including product browsing, checkout, and payment processing, to ensure everything works smoothly.

Launch your store: Once you're satisfied with your store's functionality and appearance, make it live and start promoting it to your target audience.

Section 4.5: Tips for a Successful E-commerce Store

To optimize your online store and increase the chances of success, consider the following tips:

Prioritize user experience: Ensure your store is easy to navigate, loads quickly, and offers a seamless checkout process to encourage customers to complete their purchases.

Use high-quality product images and descriptions: Invest in professional photography and well-written descriptions to showcase your products effectively and provide customers with the information they need to make a purchase.

Optimize for mobile devices: With more customers shopping on smartphones and tablets, it's essential to ensure your store is responsive and easy to use on various screen sizes.

Implement SEO best practices: Optimize your store's content, metadata, and structure to improve its visibility in search engine results.

Encourage customer reviews: Positive reviews can help build trust with potential customers and improve your store's credibility.

Offer exceptional customer support: Provide responsive, helpful customer service to address any issues or questions your customers may have.

Monitor and analyze your store's performance: Use analytics tools to track your store's performance, identify areas for improvement, and make data-driven decisions to enhance its effectiveness.

Section 4.6: Conclusion

Selecting the right e-commerce store builder is crucial to your online store's success. By considering factors such as your technical expertise, product catalog size, budget, and desired customization level, you can choose a platform that best suits your business's unique needs. Once you've selected a store builder, follow the steps outlined in this chapter to set up, customize, and launch your online store. By prioritizing user experience, optimizing for mobile devices and search engines, and offering exceptional customer support, you'll be well on your way to building a thriving e-commerce business.

WEBSITE SECURITY

Website security is a critical component of any online business, as it ensures the protection of sensitive data and builds trust with your customers. In this chapter, we'll explore website security systems, discuss their importance, and provide guidance on selecting the right one for your business. We'll also provide an overview of popular options such as Cloudflare, Akamai, and Amazon CloudFront.

Section 5.1: The Importance of Website Security Systems

A website security system is a set of tools, protocols, and practices that protect your website from various cyber threats, such as hacking, malware, data breaches, and Distributed Denial of Service (DDoS) attacks. Implementing a robust security system is crucial for several reasons:

Protect sensitive data: Your website may collect and store sensitive data, such as customer information, payment details, and login credentials. A security system helps protect this data from unauthorized access or theft.

Maintain your reputation: A security breach can damage your business's reputation, leading to lost customers and reduced trust.

Ensure website availability: Cyberattacks, such as DDoS attacks, can make your website unavailable to users. A security system helps prevent downtime and ensures your site remains accessible.

Comply with regulations: Many industries have specific regulations and standards for data protection and privacy, such as GDPR and PCI DSS. A comprehensive security system helps your business stay compliant.

Section 5.2: Choosing a Website Security System for Your Business

When selecting a website security system, consider the following factors:

Your website's size and complexity: The security needs of a small blog will differ from those of a large e-commerce store. Evaluate your website's specific requirements and choose a security system that can address them.

Your level of technical expertise: Some security systems require more technical knowledge to set up and manage than others. Consider your own technical capabilities when making your choice.

Integration with your existing infrastructure: Ensure the security system you choose is compatible with your website's platform, hosting provider, and other tools you use.

Budget: Website security systems come with varying price tags. Determine your budget and select a system that provides the best value for your investment.

Section 5.3: Overview of Popular Website Security Systems

In this section, we'll provide an overview of three popular website security systems: Cloudflare, Akamai, and Amazon CloudFront.

Cloudflare: Cloudflare is a widely used security system that offers a range of features, such as DDoS protection, web application firewall (WAF), content delivery network (CDN), and SSL encryption. Cloudflare's global network helps improve your website's performance and provides robust security against a variety of threats. Its user-friendly interface and flexible pricing plans make it suitable for businesses of all sizes.

Akamai: Akamai is a comprehensive security system that provides advanced threat protection, CDN, and performance optimization services. Its features include a WAF, DDoS protection, bot management, and API protection. Akamai's extensive network and advanced security features make it an excellent choice for large enterprises or businesses with complex security requirements. However, it may be less suitable for smaller businesses or those with limited budgets.

Amazon CloudFront: Amazon CloudFront is a CDN and security system offered by Amazon Web Services (AWS). It integrates seamlessly with other AWS services and provides features such as DDoS protection, SSL encryption, and Amazon Web Application Firewall. CloudFront is a good option for businesses already using AWS or those looking for a scalable, pay-as-you-go pricing model. However, its management and configuration may require more technical expertise than other options.

Section 5.4: Getting Started with Your Chosen Website Security System

Once you've selected a website security system that aligns with your business needs, follow these steps to set up and configure your security system:

Sign up for an account: Register for an account with your chosen security system provider, and select a pricing plan that meets your requirements.

Configure your domain: Add your domain to the security system, and update your domain's DNS settings as required by the provider. This process may vary depending on the specific system you choose.

Set up SSL encryption: Ensure that your website uses SSL encryption to protect data transmitted between your server and your users' browsers. Most security systems provide built-in SSL certificate management, making this process straightforward.

Configure the Web Application Firewall (WAF): Set up a WAF to protect your website from common web-based threats, such as SQL injections, cross-site scripting (XSS), and other vulnerabilities. Customize the WAF rules to fit your website's specific needs and risk profile.

Enable DDoS protection: Activate DDoS protection features to help safeguard your website from DDoS attacks that could disrupt its availability.

Set up monitoring and alerts: Configure monitoring tools and alerts to notify you of any security incidents or potential threats. This enables you to respond quickly and minimize potential damage.

Regularly update and maintain your security system: Ensure that your security system is always up-to-date with the latest features and patches. Regular maintenance will help to keep your website secure and running smoothly.

Section 5.5: Additional Security Best Practices

In addition to implementing a robust website security system, consider the following security best practices to further safeguard your online presence:

Keep your website software and plugins up-to-date: Regularly update your website's platform, plugins, and themes to protect against known vulnerabilities.

Use strong, unique passwords: Encourage the use of strong, unique passwords for all user accounts, including administrators and customers.

Implement two-factor authentication (2FA): Add an extra layer of security by requiring users to provide a second form of identification, such as a code sent via SMS or a mobile app.

Regularly back up your website: Create regular backups of your website, including all files and databases, to help minimize data loss in case of a security incident.

Educate your team: Train your employees about online security best practices, such as recognizing phishing emails and using secure connections when accessing sensitive data.

Section 5.6: Conclusion

Website security is a critical aspect of running an online business. By selecting the right security system for your website and implementing additional best practices, you can protect your business from cyber threats, maintain your reputation, and ensure the privacy and safety of your customers' data. Stay vigilant, regularly update and maintain your security system, and continue to educate yourself and your team on emerging threats and best practices to keep your digital fortress strong.

CRM SYSTEMS

Customer Relationship Management (CRM) systems play a vital role in managing and nurturing your business's relationships with customers and prospects. In this chapter, we'll explore what CRM systems are, their importance, and how to choose the right one for your business. We'll provide an overview of popular CRM systems, including Go High Level, Pipedrive, Salesforce, Zoho, and HubSpot, and discuss industry-specific options as well.

Section 6.1: What are CRM Systems?

CRM systems are software platforms designed to help businesses manage customer interactions, track leads, sales opportunities, and customer issues. These systems centralize customer data, making it easier for your team to access and analyze important information. Key features of CRM systems include:

Contact management: Store and organize contact information, such as names, addresses, phone numbers, and email addresses, for easy access.

Lead tracking: Track leads through the sales funnel, from initial contact to conversion.

Sales pipeline management: Monitor the progress of sales opportunities and prioritize high-potential deals.

Communication tracking: Record and track customer interactions, including emails, phone calls, meetings, and social media interactions.

Task management: Assign tasks to team members, set deadlines, and track progress.

Reporting and analytics: Generate reports and visualize data to make informed decisions and improve sales performance.

Section 6.2: The Importance of CRM Systems

CRM systems offer several benefits for businesses, including:

Improved customer relationships: By centralizing customer data and interactions, CRM systems allow your team to better understand customer needs and preferences, leading to stronger relationships and increased customer satisfaction.

Enhanced communication and collaboration: CRM systems provide a unified platform for team members to access and share customer information, ensuring that everyone is on the same page.

Increased sales productivity: CRM systems automate repetitive tasks and streamline sales processes, freeing up time for your sales team to focus on high-value activities.

Informed decision-making: CRM systems provide valuable insights and analytics, helping you identify trends and make data-driven decisions.

Section 6.3: Choosing the Right CRM System for Your Business

When selecting a CRM system for your business, consider the following factors:

Your business's size and industry: Different CRM systems cater to various business sizes and industries. Choose a system that aligns with your business's specific requirements and can be tailored to your industry.

Features and customization: Identify the features you need in a CRM system and ensure the platform you choose offers those features or can be customized to include them.

Integration with existing tools: Ensure the CRM system you select integrates seamlessly with your existing software and tools, such as email, marketing automation, and accounting systems.

Scalability: As your business grows, your CRM system should be able to adapt and expand to accommodate your changing needs.

Budget: Determine your budget and choose a CRM system that offers the best value for your investment.

Section 6.4: Overview of Popular CRM Systems

In this section, we'll provide an overview of five popular CRM systems: Go High Level, Pipedrive, Salesforce, Zoho, and HubSpot.

Go High Level: Go High Level is an all-in-one marketing and sales platform designed for digital marketing agencies and small businesses. Its CRM features include lead tracking, sales pipeline management, and communication tracking. Additionally, Go High Level offers marketing automation, appointment scheduling, and reputation management tools.

Pipedrive: Pipedrive is a sales-focused CRM system that emphasizes simplicity and ease of use. It offers features such as sales pipeline management, contact management, and customizable sales reporting. Pipedrive is ideal for small to medium-sized businesses looking for an affordable, easy-to-use CRM solution with a focus on sales processes.

Salesforce: Salesforce is a powerful, cloud-based CRM platform suitable for businesses of all sizes and industries. It offers a wide range of features, including contact management, lead tracking, sales pipeline management, and advanced reporting and analytics. Salesforce also provides a robust ecosystem of integrations and customizations, making it highly adaptable to your business's specific needs.

Zoho: Zoho CRM is a comprehensive CRM system with a broad array of features, such as contact management, sales pipeline management, lead tracking, and reporting. Zoho also offers a suite of other business tools, such as project management, accounting, and marketing automation, making it an attractive option for businesses seeking an integrated solution.

HubSpot: HubSpot CRM is a user-friendly platform designed for small to medium-sized businesses. It provides essential CRM features, such as contact management, lead tracking, and sales pipeline management. HubSpot also offers marketing, sales, and customer service tools as part of its suite of products, enabling seamless integration and collaboration across your organization.

Section 6.5: Industry-Specific CRM Systems

In addition to the general CRM systems mentioned above, there are industry-specific CRM systems tailored to the unique needs of specific sectors. After familiarizing yourself with the CRM landscape and understanding your business's requirements, we encourage you to research industry-specific options to find the perfect fit for your organization.

Some examples of industry-specific CRM systems include:

Real Estate: Propertybase, Follow Up Boss, and Wise Agent
Healthcare: Salesforce Health Cloud, Kareo, and NextGen Healthcare
Nonprofits: Blackbaud CRM, Neon CRM, and DonorPerfect

Section 6.6: Getting Started with Your CRM System

Once you've chosen the right CRM system for your business, follow these steps to get started and make the most of your new tool:

Sign up and set up your account: Register for an account with your chosen CRM provider and select the appropriate pricing plan for your business. Complete any necessary onboarding tasks, such as adding users, setting user permissions, and customizing your account settings.

Import your existing customer data: Import your current customer data into the CRM system. This may include contact information, sales history, and any relevant notes or tags. Most CRM systems offer data import tools that allow you to easily transfer information from spreadsheets or other CRM platforms.

Customize your CRM system: Tailor your CRM system to fit your business's unique needs by customizing fields, adding custom modules, and configuring workflows. This will help you streamline your processes and ensure the CRM system aligns with your specific requirements.

Integrate with other tools: Connect your CRM system with other tools and software your business uses, such as email, marketing automation, project management, and accounting systems. This will enable seamless data flow and improve overall efficiency across your organization.

Train your team: Provide comprehensive training for your team members to ensure they understand how to use the CRM system effectively. This may include attending vendor-provided training sessions, watching video tutorials, or participating in hands-on workshops.

Define and implement processes: Establish clear processes and guidelines for using the CRM system, such as data entry standards, lead management processes, and sales pipeline stages. This will help ensure consistency and accuracy across your team.

Monitor and evaluate performance: Regularly review your CRM system's performance and evaluate its impact on your business. Analyze reports and metrics to identify areas for improvement and make any necessary adjustments to your processes or CRM configuration.

Continuously optimize your CRM system: As your business evolves, your CRM system should adapt to meet your changing needs. Continually refine your CRM configuration, add new features or integrations, and stay up-to-date with the latest best practices to maximize the system's value for your organization.

Section 6.7: Conclusion

Implementing a CRM system is a significant investment in your business's success. By following these steps to get started, you'll lay the foundation for an efficient, data-driven approach to managing customer relationships and improving sales performance. Remember to keep your CRM system up-to-date, provide ongoing training for your team, and continuously optimize your processes to ensure your CRM system remains a valuable asset for your business.

BUSINESS EMAIL/SMTP

In this chapter, we'll explore Business Email and SMTP systems, their importance, and how to choose the right one for your business. We'll provide an overview of popular options, including Google Workspace, Microsoft 365, Zoho Workplace, Amazon SES, SendGrid, Mailgun, and SendinBlue. Additionally, we'll discuss getting started with your chosen system, avoiding spam, and integrating it with your CRM system.

Section 7.1: What are Business Email and SMTP Systems?

A Business Email system is a professional email service designed specifically for businesses, offering features like custom domain names, larger storage, and advanced security options. An SMTP (Simple Mail Transfer Protocol) system, on the other hand, is a service that enables the sending of bulk or transactional emails from your applications, websites, or CRM systems.

While some providers offer both business email and SMTP services, others specialize in one or the other.

It's important to understand the distinctions between these services and choose a provider that meets your specific needs.

Section 7.2: The Importance of Business Email and SMTP Systems

Business Email and SMTP systems offer several benefits, including:

Professionalism: Custom domain names in your email address convey a professional image, building trust and credibility with customers and partners.

Scalability: Business email and SMTP systems can handle large volumes of emails, making them suitable for growing businesses.

Security and privacy: These systems offer advanced security features, such as encryption and spam protection, to safeguard your communications and sensitive information.

Integration: Business email and SMTP systems can be integrated with other business tools, such as CRM systems, to streamline communication and improve efficiency.

Section 7.3: Choosing the Right Business Email and SMTP System for Your Business

When selecting a business email and SMTP system, consider the following factors:

Features: Identify the features you need, such as storage capacity, custom domain names, and advanced security options.

Reliability: Choose a provider with a reputation for reliable and consistent email delivery.

Integration: Ensure the system integrates seamlessly with your existing tools, such as CRM systems and email clients.

Scalability: Select a system that can grow with your business, accommodating increased email volumes and additional users.

Budget: Determine your budget and choose a system that offers the best value for your investment.

Section 7.4: Overview of Popular Business Email and SMTP Systems

In this section, we'll provide an overview of popular business email and SMTP systems, including Google Workspace, Microsoft 365, Zoho Workplace, Amazon SES, SendGrid, Mailgun, and SendinBlue.

Google Workspace: Google Workspace is a suite of productivity and collaboration tools, including Gmail for business email. It offers custom domain names, ample storage, and integration with other Google services, such as Google Drive and Google Meet.

Microsoft 365: Microsoft 365 is a suite of productivity tools, including Outlook for business email. It provides custom domain names, large storage capacity, and integration with other Microsoft applications, such as Word, Excel, and Teams.

Zoho Workplace: Zoho Workplace is an integrated suite of productivity and collaboration tools, including Zoho Mail for business email. It offers custom domain names, generous storage, and seamless integration with other Zoho apps.

Amazon SES (SMTP): Amazon Simple Email Service (SES) is a cloud-based SMTP system designed for sending bulk and transactional emails. It provides high deliverability, scalability, and integration with other AWS services.

SendGrid (SMTP): SendGrid is a cloud-based SMTP service focused on delivering transactional and marketing emails. It offers a user-friendly interface, high deliverability, and advanced analytics. SendGrid also provides email template management and an API for integration with other systems.

Mailgun (SMTP): Mailgun is a cloud-based SMTP service designed for developers and businesses sending transactional emails. It offers high deliverability, powerful email analytics, and an API for seamless integration with other tools.

SendinBlue: SendinBlue is a marketing and transactional email service that offers both business email and SMTP capabilities. It provides custom domain names, advanced analytics, and a wide range of email marketing features, such as templates, automation, and segmentation.

Section 7.5: Getting Started with Your Chosen Business Email and SMTP System

Once you've selected a business email and SMTP system, follow these steps to get started:

Sign up for an account: Register for an account with your chosen provider and select the appropriate pricing plan for your business.

Set up your custom domain: Configure your custom domain with your email provider, following their guidelines for domain verification and DNS settings.

Create email accounts: Set up email accounts for your team members, assigning appropriate roles and permissions.

Configure SMTP settings: If using an SMTP system, configure your SMTP settings within your applications, websites, or CRM systems, following your provider's documentation.

Train your team: Ensure your team members are familiar with the email system's features and functionality, providing training or resources as needed.

Section 7.6: Avoiding Spam and Ensuring Deliverability

To ensure your emails reach their intended recipients and avoid being marked as spam, follow these best practices:

Authenticate your emails: Set up SPF, DKIM, and DMARC records in your domain's DNS settings to authenticate your emails, proving they come from a trusted sender.

Maintain a clean email list: Regularly update your email list, removing bounced addresses, inactive subscribers, and unengaged contacts.

Personalize your emails: Use personalization tokens and dynamic content to make your emails more relevant and engaging for recipients.

Monitor your sender reputation: Keep an eye on your sender reputation, which is affected by factors such as spam complaints, bounce rates, and email engagement. A high sender reputation increases the likelihood of your emails reaching the inbox.

Section 7.7: Integrating Your Business Email and SMTP System with Your CRM

To streamline communication and improve efficiency, integrate your business email and SMTP system with your CRM:

Configure email settings: In your CRM system, configure the email settings to connect with your chosen business email or SMTP provider, following the provider's documentation.

Sync contacts and leads: Ensure your CRM contacts and leads are synced with your email system, enabling you to send targeted and personalized emails.

Set up email templates and automation: Create email templates within your CRM system for common communications, and set up automation rules to trigger emails based on specific actions or events.

Monitor email performance: Use your CRM system's reporting and analytics features to monitor the performance of your email campaigns, enabling you to optimize your email strategy.

Section 7.8: Conclusion

Business email and SMTP systems are essential tools for effective communication and email marketing. By selecting the right provider, setting up your system properly, and integrating it with your CRM, you can ensure a professional, efficient, and scalable email solution for your business.

SOCIAL MEDIA MANAGEMENT SOFTWARE

In this chapter, we'll explore Social Media Management Software, their functions, and how to choose the right one for your business. We'll provide an overview of popular options, including Cloud Campaign, SocialPilot, Buffer, MeetEdgar, and Zoho Social. Additionally, we'll discuss getting started with your chosen software.

Section 8.1: What is Social Media Management Software?

Social Media Management Software is a tool that helps businesses manage their social media presence across multiple platforms. These tools typically offer features such as post scheduling, content curation, analytics, and collaboration, streamlining the process of planning, executing, and monitoring social media campaigns.

Section 8.2: Functions of Social Media Management Software

Social Media Management Software offers several key functions, including:

Post scheduling: Schedule social media posts across multiple platforms, ensuring consistency and optimal timing for your content.

Content curation: Discover and curate relevant content from various sources to share on your social media channels.

Analytics: Track the performance of your social media campaigns, identifying key metrics such as engagement, reach, and conversions.

Collaboration: Collaborate with team members on content creation, approval, and scheduling, promoting a cohesive social media strategy.

Social listening: Monitor social media conversations and mentions of your brand, enabling you to respond to customer inquiries and engage with your audience.

Section 8.3: Choosing the Right Social Media Management Software for Your Business

When selecting Social Media Management Software, consider the following factors:

Supported platforms: Ensure the software supports all the social media platforms your business uses.

Features: Identify the features you need, such as post scheduling, content curation, analytics, and collaboration.

Ease of use: Choose a user-friendly tool that can be easily adopted by your team members.

Scalability: Select a tool that can grow with your business, accommodating increased social media activity and additional users.

Budget: Determine your budget and choose a tool that offers the best value for your investment.

Section 8.4: Overview of Popular Social Media Management Software

In this section, we'll provide an overview of popular Social Media Management Software, including Cloud Campaign, SocialPilot, Buffer, MeetEdgar, and Zoho Social.

Cloud Campaign: Cloud Campaign is a powerful social media management tool designed for agencies and businesses. It offers features such as post scheduling, content curation, analytics, and collaboration. Cloud Campaign also provides white-labeling options for agencies looking to offer social media management services under their brand.

SocialPilot: SocialPilot is a user-friendly social media management tool that supports post scheduling, content curation, analytics, and collaboration. It also offers social media calendar and team management features, making it ideal for businesses with multiple team members.

Buffer: Buffer is a popular social media management tool that simplifies post scheduling and content curation. It offers a clean, intuitive interface, making it easy for users to plan and execute their social media campaigns. Buffer also provides analytics and integration with other marketing tools.

MeetEdgar: MeetEdgar is a social media management tool with a focus on content recycling and automation. It automatically schedules and reshares your evergreen content, ensuring your social media channels remain active with minimal effort. MeetEdgar also offers content curation and analytics features.

Zoho Social: Zoho Social is part of the Zoho Workplace suite, offering post scheduling, content curation, analytics, and collaboration. It seamlessly integrates with other Zoho applications, such as Zoho CRM, making it a convenient option for businesses already using the Zoho ecosystem.

Section 8.5: Getting Started with Your Chosen Social Media Management Software

Once you've selected a Social Media Management Software, follow these steps to get started:

Sign up for an account: Register for an account with your chosen software provider and select the appropriate pricing plan for your business.

Connect your social media accounts: Link your social media accounts to the software, granting the necessary permissions for it to manage your social media presence.

Familiarize yourself with the interface: Spend some time exploring the software's features and user interface, ensuring you understand how to navigate and utilize its functions effectively.

Create and schedule content: Begin creating content for your social media channels, using the software's scheduling and content curation features to plan your social media campaigns.

Set up team collaboration: If your chosen software offers team collaboration features, invite your team members and set up appropriate roles and permissions to streamline your social media management process.

Monitor your analytics: Regularly review the analytics provided by your software to gauge the performance of your social media campaigns, making adjustments as needed to optimize your strategy.

Engage with your audience: Use the social listening and engagement features of your software to respond to comments, messages, and mentions, fostering a strong connection with your audience.

Section 8.6: Conclusion

Social Media Management Software can significantly simplify and streamline your social media marketing efforts. By choosing the right tool for your business and effectively utilizing its features, you can efficiently manage your social media presence, engage with your audience, and ultimately drive better results for your business.

CONTENT CREATION TOOLS

Have you ever wished you could have a utility belt like Batman or any other superhero? Well, the good news is that you don't need to be a caped crusader to have a digital utility belt. In the digital age, content creation has become a crucial element of any business, organization or individual looking to make an impact online. Whether you're creating written content, graphics, videos, or podcasts, having the right tools at your disposal is essential to make your content stand out in the sea of information that's available online.

In this chapter of Digital Utility Belt, we'll explore a range of content creation tools that are essential for any aspiring content creator. From content research tools that help you find the right keywords and topics to graphic design tools that enable you to create stunning visuals, we'll cover a wide range of tools that will make your content creation process smoother and more efficient. We'll also take a look at video editing tools that can help you create professional-quality videos, written content tools that can help you improve your writing, and podcast and audio editing tools that can help you produce high-quality audio content.

But that's not all. We'll also explore royalty-free resources that you can use to enhance your content, as well as content automation tools that can help you streamline your content creation process. With the right digital utility belt, you'll be able to create content like a pro and stand out in the crowded online space.

So, buckle up and get ready to explore some of the most powerful content creation tools available. With the right tools at your fingertips, you'll be well on your way to creating content that's worthy of a superhero's utility belt.

CONTENT PLANNING TOOLS

In this section, we'll discuss Content Planning and Research tools, their importance, and provide an overview of popular tools such as SEMrush Keyword Magic Tool, Google Trends, SEMrush Topic Research Tool, AlsoAsked, AnswerThePublic, BuzzSumo, Pinterest Trends, and Chat GPT. We'll also include a brief guide on getting started with each tool.

Section 9.1.1: Why are Content Planning and Research Tools Important?

Content planning and research tools are essential for any successful content marketing strategy. These tools help you:

- Identify trending topics and keywords relevant to your target audience.
- Understand user intent and search patterns.
- Discover content gaps and opportunities.
- Analyze competitors' content strategies.
- Generate content ideas and inspiration.

By utilizing these tools, you can create compelling, data-driven content that resonates with your audience and drives engagement, traffic, and conversions.

Section 9.1.2: Overview of Popular Content Planning and Research Tools

SEMrush Keyword Magic Tool: This tool helps you discover and analyze keywords for your content strategy. It provides valuable data such as search volume, keyword difficulty, and related keywords.

Google Trends: Google Trends shows the popularity of search queries over time, helping you identify trending topics and seasonal patterns.

SEMrush Topic Research Tool: This tool helps you generate content ideas based on trending topics, user questions, and competitors' content.

AlsoAsked: AlsoAsked is a free tool that provides insights into related questions people ask on search engines, helping you create content that answers those questions.

AnswerThePublic: AnswerThePublic is a visual keyword research tool that generates questions, prepositions, and comparisons related to your seed keyword.

BuzzSumo: BuzzSumo is a content research and analysis tool that helps you discover the most shared and engaged-with content across social media platforms.

Pinterest Trends: Pinterest Trends provides insights into popular and trending searches on Pinterest, offering a unique perspective on visual content ideas.

Chat GPT: Chat GPT is an AI-powered language model that can help you brainstorm content ideas and even generate content drafts.

Section 9.1.3: Conclusion

Content planning and research tools are invaluable for creating a data-driven content strategy that resonates with your target audience. By leveraging these tools, you can discover trending topics, generate content ideas, and analyze competitors, ultimately producing content that drives engagement and conversions.

GRAPHIC DESIGN TOOLS

In this section, we'll discuss Graphic Design tools, their importance, and provide an overview of popular tools such as Canva, Adobe Photoshop, GIMP, Inkscape, Vectr, Adobe Illustrator, Procreate, Affinity Designer, Adobe Express, AutoEnhance.ai, and LunaPic. We'll also separate the tools by free options and paid/premium software.

Section 9.2.1: Why are Graphic Design Tools Important?

Graphic design tools are essential for creating visually appealing content that attracts and engages your target audience. These tools help you:

- Create and edit images, logos, and illustrations for your website, social media, and marketing materials.
- Maintain consistent branding through the use of templates, color palettes, and typography.

- Enhance the visual appeal of your content, making it more shareable and memorable.
- Save time and resources by streamlining the design process.
- Section 9.2.2: Overview of Popular Graphic Design Tools

Free Options:

Canva: A user-friendly online design tool offering templates, images, and design elements to create social media graphics, presentations, and more.

GIMP: A free, open-source image editor that offers a range of features for photo retouching, image composition, and image authoring.

Inkscape: A free, open-source vector graphics editor with capabilities similar to Adobe Illustrator.

Vectr: A free, web-based vector graphics editor that's easy to use and offers real-time collaboration features.

Adobe Express: A free, online photo editing tool that offers basic image editing features and templates for creating social media graphics.

LunaPic: A free, online photo editor with a variety of basic editing features and effects.

AutoEnhance.ai: An AI-powered image enhancement tool that automatically improves the quality of your photos with features such as color correction, noise reduction, and sharpness.

Paid/Premium Software:

Adobe Photoshop: A powerful, industry-standard image editing software that offers advanced features for photo retouching, graphic design, and digital art.

Adobe Illustrator: A professional vector graphics editor that offers advanced features for creating logos, illustrations, and typography.

Procreate: A popular, iPad-exclusive drawing app that offers a range of features for creating digital art, illustrations, and animations.

Affinity Designer: A professional vector graphics editor that offers powerful features and a more affordable one-time payment option compared to Adobe Illustrator.

Mockup.photos: Mockup Photos collects high quality mockup images from around the world. Use Mockup Photos to generate app screenshots in seconds.

Section 9.2.3: Conclusion

Graphic design tools are crucial for creating visually appealing and engaging content for your audience. By selecting the right tool for your needs, whether it's a free option or a paid/premium software, you can streamline your design process and elevate the visual quality of your content. Ensure you consider your design needs, budget, and skill level when choosing the appropriate tool for your business.

VIDEO EDITING TOOLS

In this section, we'll discuss Video Editing Software, their importance, and provide an overview of popular tools such as Descript, Canva, Loom, Headliner, Adobe Premiere Pro, Filmora, and CapCut. We'll also include tips for getting started with each tool.

Section 9.3.1: Why are Video Editing Software Important?

Video editing software is crucial for creating engaging video content that captures the attention of your audience. These tools help you:

- Edit and enhance raw video footage, transforming it into polished content.
- Add effects, transitions, and animations to make your videos more engaging.
- Create professional-quality videos for marketing, educational, or entertainment purposes.
- Optimize your videos for various platforms and devices.
- By using the right video editing software, you can create high-quality videos that resonate with your audience and drive engagement, traffic, and conversions.

Section 9.3.2: Overview of Popular Video Editing Software

Descript: Descript is a unique video editing software that uses AI-powered transcription to edit video and audio files using text.

Canva: Canva offers a video editing feature that allows you to create simple videos using templates, stock footage, and various design elements.

Loom: Loom is a video recording and sharing platform that enables you to create quick screen recordings, presentations, and video messages.

Headliner: Headliner is an online video editing tool designed for creating social media videos, podcasts, and audiograms.

Adobe Premiere Pro: Adobe Premiere Pro is a professional video editing software that offers advanced features for creating high-quality videos, films, and TV shows.

Filmora: Filmora is a user-friendly video editing software with a range of features for creating and enhancing videos for various purposes.
Getting Started: Purchase and download Filmora, install the software on your computer, and explore the interface and tools to start editing your videos.

CapCut: CapCut is a mobile video editing app that offers easy-to-use features for creating and editing videos on the go.

Section 9.3.3: Conclusion

Video editing software is essential for creating engaging and professional video content that connects with your audience. By selecting the right tool for your needs and effectively utilizing its features, you can produce high-quality videos that drive engagement and conversions. Consider factors such as your budget, skill level, and video requirements when choosing the appropriate video editing software for your business.

WRITTEN CONTENT TOOLS

In this section, we'll discuss Written Content Creation Tools, their importance, and provide an overview of popular tools such as Chat GPT, Grammarly, Hemingway App, SEMrush SEO Writing Assistant, Yoast, and ProWritingAid.

Section 9.4.1: Why are Written Content Creation Tools Important?

Written content creation tools are essential for producing high-quality written content that engages your audience and effectively communicates your message. These tools help you:

- Improve the quality and readability of your writing by identifying and correcting grammar, spelling, and punctuation errors.
- Enhance your content's SEO by optimizing it for relevant keywords and readability.

- Streamline the writing process by providing suggestions and recommendations based on best practices.
- Save time and resources by automating various aspects of the content creation process.
- By using the right written content creation tools, you can create compelling content that resonates with your audience and drives engagement, traffic, and conversions.

Section 9.4.2: Overview of Popular Written Content Creation Tools

Chat GPT: Chat GPT is an AI-powered writing assistant that can help you generate ideas, write articles, and create various types of content.

Grammarly: Grammarly is a widely-used writing assistant that checks for grammar, spelling, punctuation, and style errors in real-time and provides suggestions for improvement.

Hemingway App: Hemingway App is an online writing editor that focuses on improving the readability of your content by highlighting complex sentences, passive voice, and adverbs.

SEMrush SEO Writing Assistant: The SEMrush SEO Writing Assistant is an online tool that helps you optimize your content for SEO by providing keyword recommendations, readability scores, and more.

Yoast: Yoast is a popular WordPress plugin that helps you optimize your content for SEO by providing real-time suggestions and feedback.

ProWritingAid: ProWritingAid is a comprehensive writing assistant that checks for grammar, style, and readability issues, and provides suggestions for improvement.

Section 9.4.3: Conclusion

Written content creation tools are vital for producing high-quality, engaging, and SEO-optimized content that connects with your audience. By selecting the right tools for your needs and effectively utilizing their features, you can create compelling content that drives engagement and conversions. Consider factors such as your budget, writing requirements, and desired level of automation when choosing the appropriate content creation tools for your business.

PODCAST AND AUDIO EDITTING

In this section, we'll discuss Audio Content Editors, their importance, and provide an overview of popular tools such as Audacity, GarageBand, Adobe Audition, Logic Pro, Riverside.fm, and Anchor.

Section 9.5.1: Why are Audio Content Editors Important?

Audio content editors are essential for producing high-quality audio content such as podcasts, audiobooks, and voiceovers. These tools help you:

- Edit and enhance raw audio recordings, removing unwanted noise and improving the overall quality.
- Add effects, transitions, and background music to create engaging and professional audio content.
- Record, mix, and master audio content for various platforms and devices.
- Streamline the audio editing process by providing an intuitive user interface and advanced features.
- By using the right audio content editor, you can create captivating audio content that resonates with your audience and drives engagement, traffic, and conversions.

Section 9.5.2: Overview of Popular Audio Content Editors

Audacity: Audacity is a free, open-source audio editing software that offers a wide range of features for recording, editing, and exporting audio content.

GarageBand: GarageBand is a user-friendly audio editing software available for macOS and iOS devices, allowing you to create music, podcasts, and other audio content.

Adobe Audition: Adobe Audition is a professional audio editing software that offers advanced features for creating, editing, and mastering high-quality audio content.

Logic Pro: Logic Pro is a powerful digital audio workstation (DAW) designed for macOS, offering advanced features for music production, mixing, and mastering.

Riverside.fm: Riverside.fm is an online platform that enables you to record high-quality podcasts and interviews remotely, providing separate audio and video tracks for easy editing.

Anchor: Anchor is an all-in-one podcast creation platform that allows you to record, edit, and distribute your podcasts across various platforms.

Section 9.5.3: Conclusion

Audio content editors are crucial for creating engaging and professional audio content that connects with your audience. By selecting the right tool for your needs and effectively utilizing its features, you can produce high-quality audio content that drives engagement and conversions. Consider factors such as your budget, skill level, and audio requirements when choosing the appropriate audio content editor for your business.

ROYALTY-FREE RESOURCES

In this section, we will discuss royalty-free resources, their importance to business owners, and provide an overview of popular platforms, including Pexels, Unsplash, Pixabay, Epidemic Sound, YouTube and CapCut music libraries, Envato Elements, Artlist.io, and Shutterstock.

Section 9.6.1: Why are Royalty-Free Resources Important for Business Owners?

Royalty-free resources are crucial for business owners for several reasons:

Legal compliance: Using copyrighted material without permission can result in legal issues and hefty fines. Royalty-free resources ensure that you can use the content without worrying about copyright infringement.

Cost-effective: Royalty-free resources are often available at a fraction of the cost of copyrighted content, making them an affordable option for businesses of all sizes.

Time-saving: Searching for and obtaining permissions for copyrighted material can be time-consuming. Royalty-free resources provide quick access to a vast library of content, allowing you to focus on other aspects of your business.

Enhance your content: High-quality royalty-free resources can elevate your content, making it more engaging and visually appealing to your audience.

Section 9.6.2: Overview of Popular Royalty-Free Resources

Pexels: Pexels offers a vast collection of high-quality, royalty-free stock photos and videos. The platform is entirely free and requires no attribution for most uses.

Unsplash: Unsplash is a popular platform for finding beautiful, high-resolution, royalty-free images. The images are free to use for both personal and commercial projects.

Pixabay: Pixabay is a platform that provides access to over 2 million royalty-free stock photos, illustrations, vectors, and videos, all free for commercial use without the need for attribution.

Epidemic Sound: Epidemic Sound offers a large library of royalty-free music and sound effects. The platform requires a subscription but provides access to a wide range of high-quality audio content.

YouTube and CapCut Music Libraries: Both YouTube and CapCut offer built-in music libraries with royalty-free music tracks that you can use in your video projects without any copyright issues.

Envato Elements: Envato Elements is a subscription-based service that provides access to a vast library of royalty-free stock photos, videos, music, graphics, templates, and more.

Artlist.io: Artlist.io is a subscription-based platform offering royalty-free music and sound effects for use in video and audio projects, with a license that covers both personal and commercial use.

Shutterstock: Shutterstock is a well-known platform for accessing a vast collection of royalty-free stock photos, videos, illustrations, vectors, and music tracks. The platform requires a subscription or pay-per-image pricing.

Section 9.6.3: Conclusion

Royalty-free resources play a crucial role in helping business owners create engaging and visually appealing content while avoiding copyright issues. By utilizing the platforms mentioned above, you can find high-quality resources to enhance your content without breaking the bank or compromising legal compliance. Remember to review the specific terms and conditions of each platform to ensure you are using the resources correctly and within the bounds of their respective licenses.

REPURPOSE.IO

In this section, we will discuss Repurpose.io, what it is, how it can be helpful to business owners, and how to get started with it.

Section 9.7.1: What is Repurpose.io?

Repurpose.io is a content repurposing tool that allows you to automatically convert your content into various formats and distribute it across different platforms. With Repurpose.io, you can easily turn your podcast episodes into videos, blog posts into social media posts, and more. This powerful tool helps you maximize your content's reach and engagement by reusing and repackaging it for different audiences and platforms.

Section 9.7.2: How Can Repurpose.io Be Helpful to Business Owners?

Repurpose.io offers several benefits to business owners, including:

Increased reach and engagement: By repurposing your content into different formats, you can reach a wider audience and increase engagement across various platforms.

Time and resource savings: Repurpose.io automates the content repurposing process, saving you time and resources that can be better spent on other aspects of your business.

Improved SEO: Repurposing your content allows you to target different keywords and improve your website's search engine optimization (SEO).

Enhanced brand visibility: By consistently publishing repurposed content across multiple platforms, you increase your brand visibility and establish yourself as an industry expert.

Extended content lifespan: Repurposing your content gives it a longer lifespan, allowing you to continue benefiting from its value over time.

Section 9.7.3: Getting Started with Repurpose.io

To get started with Repurpose.io, follow these steps:

Sign up: Visit the Repurpose.io website and sign up for an account. Choose a subscription plan that best suits your needs and budget.

Connect your content sources: After signing up, connect your content sources, such as your podcast hosting platform, YouTube channel, or blog, to Repurpose.io.

Set up repurposing workflows: Create workflows to define how your content should be repurposed. For example, you can set up a workflow to automatically convert your podcast episodes into video clips for YouTube or to create quote images from your blog posts for social media.

Customize your output: Repurpose.io allows you to customize your repurposed content by adding your logo, selecting a specific format or style, and more.

Schedule and publish: Once your workflows are set up, you can schedule and publish your repurposed content across different platforms automatically or manually.

Section 9.7.4: Conclusion

Repurpose.io is an invaluable tool for business owners looking to maximize their content's potential and reach a wider audience. By automating the content repurposing process, you can save time and resources while increasing engagement and brand visibility across various platforms. Start using Repurpose.io to transform your existing content into new formats and drive better results for your business.

PROJECT MANAGEMENT AND PRODUCTIVITY SOFTWARE

In this chapter, we will explore project management and productivity tools, including Trello, ClickUp, Asana, Podio, and Monday.com. We will also offer tips on implementing a productivity system and committing to it, whether you are a solopreneur or part of a large team.

Section 10.1: Overview of Project Management and Productivity Tools

Trello: Trello is a visual project management tool that uses boards, lists, and cards to help you organize and prioritize tasks. It's intuitive and easy to use, making it ideal for both small teams and individual users.

ClickUp: ClickUp is an all-in-one project management and productivity tool that offers a wide range of features, including task management, time tracking, goal setting, and more. With its robust customization options, it can be tailored to suit businesses of all sizes and industries.

Asana: Asana is a popular project management tool that helps teams plan, organize, and track work through tasks and subtasks. Its intuitive interface and powerful features make it ideal for both small teams and large organizations.

Podio: Podio is a flexible and customizable project management tool that enables teams to collaborate, communicate, and get work done in one place. With its wide range of integrations and customizable apps, Podio is suitable for businesses of all sizes.

Monday.com: Monday.com is a work operating system that allows teams to manage tasks, projects, and workflows in a highly visual and customizable environment. With its scalable features, Monday.com is an excellent choice for businesses of all sizes, from startups to enterprises.

Section 10.2: Implementing a Productivity System as a Solopreneur

Assess your needs: Before selecting a project management tool, consider your specific needs and requirements. Determine what features are most important to you, such as task management, time tracking, or collaboration tools.

Start with a free trial: Most project management tools offer free trials or limited free plans. Take advantage of these offers to test out the platform and determine if it's the right fit for your needs.

Customize the tool to fit your workflow: Once you've chosen a tool, customize it to fit your specific workflow. This may include creating custom boards, lists, and tasks, or integrating with other tools you use in your business.

Commit to using the tool consistently: To see the benefits of a project management tool, you need to commit to using it consistently. Set aside time each day or week to update your tasks and track your progress.

Continuously evaluate and adjust: As your business evolves, your needs may change. Regularly evaluate your productivity system and make adjustments as necessary to ensure it remains effective and efficient.

Section 10.3: Implementing a Productivity System for Large Teams

Involve your team in the selection process: When choosing a project management tool for a large team, involve key team members in the decision-making process. This will help ensure the tool meets the needs of the entire team and increases buy-in.

Train your team: Once you've selected a tool, provide training to ensure all team members understand how to use it effectively. This may include group training sessions, webinars, or one-on-one support.

Establish clear guidelines and expectations: Develop clear guidelines and expectations for how the tool should be used within your team. This may include naming conventions, task assignment protocols, and communication guidelines.

Monitor progress and encourage accountability: Use the project management tool to monitor team progress and hold team members accountable for completing tasks on time. Regularly review progress and address any issues that arise.

Continuously improve: Encourage team members to provide feedback on the productivity system and make improvements as needed. Regularly reassess the effectiveness of the tool and adjust your processes to maximize efficiency and effectiveness.

Section 10.4: Tips for Committing to a Productivity System

Establish a routine: Develop a routine for updating and managing your tasks within the project management tool. Set aside dedicated time each day or week to review your tasks and adjust your priorities.

Break tasks into smaller, manageable pieces: Breaking tasks into smaller, more manageable pieces can make them less overwhelming and help you stay on track. Create subtasks or checklists within your project management tool to keep track of progress.

Use labels and tags: Use labels, tags, or categories to organize tasks and projects within your tool. This can help you quickly identify priorities and track progress.

Set deadlines and reminders: Set deadlines for tasks and use reminders to help you stay on track. Many project management tools offer built-in reminder features to help you manage your time effectively.

Collaborate and communicate: If you're working with a team, use the project management tool to collaborate and communicate effectively. Share updates, ask questions, and provide feedback within the tool to keep everyone on the same page.

Review and adjust: Regularly review your productivity system and make adjustments as needed. Be open to trying new features or techniques to improve efficiency and effectiveness.

In conclusion, project management and productivity tools can be incredibly beneficial for both solopreneurs and large teams. By selecting the right tool, customizing it to fit your workflow, and committing to using it consistently, you can greatly improve your productivity and efficiency. Remember to continuously evaluate and adjust your productivity system to ensure it remains effective as your business grows and evolves.

ACCOUNTING SOFTWARE

In this chapter, we will discuss the importance of accounting software, how to choose the right one for your business, and provide overviews of popular options like QuickBooks, Xero, and FreshBooks. Additionally, we will cover how to get started with your new accounting software.

Section 11.1: The Importance of Accounting Software

Accurate financial records: Accounting software helps businesses maintain accurate financial records, which is crucial for decision-making, budgeting, and tax compliance.

Time savings: By automating various accounting tasks such as invoicing, expense tracking, and reconciliation, accounting software saves you time and allows you to focus on other aspects of your business.

Improved cash flow management: Accounting software provides insights into your cash flow, enabling you to monitor income and expenses more effectively, identify potential issues, and make informed financial decisions.

Tax compliance: Accounting software simplifies tax compliance by helping you track income, expenses, and tax deductions, as well as generating the necessary financial reports.

Scalability: As your business grows, accounting software can be easily upgraded to accommodate increased transaction volumes and more complex financial requirements.

Section 11.2: Choosing the Right Accounting Software

Assess your needs: Before selecting accounting software, consider your business's specific needs and requirements. Determine what features are most important to you, such as invoicing, inventory management, payroll, or reporting capabilities.

Compare pricing and features: Compare the pricing and features of various accounting software options to find the one that best suits your budget and needs.

Consider ease of use and support: Look for accounting software with an intuitive interface and robust customer support to ensure a smooth implementation and ongoing use.

Integration with other tools: Choose accounting software that can integrate with your existing tools and systems, such as CRM, project management, or payment processing platforms.

Read reviews and ask for recommendations: Read online reviews and ask other business owners for their recommendations to help you choose the right accounting software for your needs.

Section 11.3: Overviews of Popular Accounting Software Options

QuickBooks: QuickBooks is a widely used accounting software that offers a range of features, including invoicing, expense tracking, payroll, and reporting. With its user-friendly interface and extensive integration options, QuickBooks is suitable for businesses of all sizes.

Xero: Xero is a cloud-based accounting software that provides a range of features, such as invoicing, bank reconciliation, inventory management, and reporting. Its intuitive interface and robust integrations make Xero a popular choice for small and medium-sized businesses.

FreshBooks: FreshBooks is a cloud-based accounting software designed for small businesses and freelancers. It offers features like invoicing, expense tracking, time tracking, and reporting. FreshBooks is known for its simplicity and ease of use, making it ideal for those new to accounting software.

Section 11.4: Getting Started with Your New Accounting Software

Sign up and choose a plan: After selecting the right accounting software for your business, sign up and choose the appropriate plan based on your needs and budget.

Set up your account: Customize your account settings, including your business name, address, tax information, and financial year start date.

Connect your bank accounts: Link your business bank accounts and credit cards to the accounting software to enable automatic transaction tracking and reconciliation.

Import existing data: If you have existing financial data, import it into your new accounting software to maintain continuity and accuracy.

Set up your chart of accounts: Customize your chart of accounts to match your business's specific financial structure, including income and expense categories, assets, and liabilities.

Configure invoicing and payment options: Set up your invoicing preferences, including custom templates, payment terms, and payment gateway integrations for easy online payments.

Integrate with other tools: Connect your accounting software with other tools you use, such as CRM, project management, or payment processing platforms, to streamline your workflow and improve efficiency.

Train your team: If you have employees who will be using the accounting software, provide them with the necessary training and resources to ensure they can use the software effectively.

Set up recurring tasks and reminders: Configure recurring tasks, such as invoicing or expense tracking, and set up reminders to help you stay on top of your financial management.

Regularly review and update your financial data: Schedule regular times to review and update your financial data in the accounting software to maintain accuracy and stay informed about your business's financial health.

In conclusion, investing in the right accounting software is essential for the financial success of your business. By understanding the importance of accounting software, assessing your specific needs, comparing popular options like QuickBooks, Xero, and FreshBooks, and implementing your chosen solution, you can improve your financial management, save time, and make informed decisions to drive your business forward.

HUMAN RESOURCE SOFTWARE

In this chapter, we will discuss what human resources software is, the different types available, how to decide which one you need, and provide overviews of popular options like Monday.com HR, Bamboo HR, Rippling, Workday, Zenefits, and more.

Section 12.1: What is Human Resources Software?

Human resources (HR) software is a digital solution designed to streamline and automate various HR tasks, including employee recruitment, onboarding, performance management, time tracking, payroll, and benefits administration. By using HR software, businesses can save time, reduce errors, and improve overall efficiency in their HR processes.

Section 12.2: Types of Human Resources Software

There are several types of HR software available, including:

All-in-one HR platforms: These comprehensive solutions cover a wide range of HR tasks, making them suitable for businesses looking for an all-encompassing solution.

Applicant tracking systems (ATS): These tools focus on streamlining the recruitment process, including job posting, applicant management, and interview scheduling.

Performance management systems: These platforms help organizations manage employee performance through goal setting, performance reviews, and feedback mechanisms.

Payroll and benefits administration systems: These tools automate payroll processes and manage employee benefits, including tax calculations, deductions, and compliance.

Time and attendance systems: These solutions track employee working hours, overtime, and time off, helping businesses manage labor costs and compliance with labor regulations.

Section 12.3: Deciding What Kind of Human Resources Software You Need

To decide which type of HR software is best for your business, consider the following:

Identify your HR needs: Assess your current HR processes and determine which areas could benefit from automation or streamlining. This will help you narrow down the type of HR software you need.

Evaluate your budget: Determine how much you can afford to spend on HR software and look for solutions that fit within your budget.

Consider your company size and growth potential: Choose an HR software that can scale with your business as it grows, ensuring you won't outgrow the system in the near future.

Look for integrations: If you're already using other business software, such as accounting or project management tools, consider HR solutions that can integrate with these systems for seamless data sharing and improved efficiency.

Test the software: Many HR software providers offer free trials or demos, allowing you to test the platform and evaluate its suitability for your business before committing to a purchase.

Section 12.4: Overviews of Popular Human Resources Software

Monday.com HR: Monday.com offers a customizable HR platform that can be tailored to meet the specific needs of your business. With modules for recruitment, onboarding, performance management, and more, Monday.com HR is suitable for businesses of all sizes.

Bamboo HR: Bamboo HR is a comprehensive HR solution designed for small and medium-sized businesses. It offers features like applicant tracking, onboarding, time tracking, and performance management. Bamboo HR is known for its user-friendly interface and robust reporting capabilities.

Rippling: Rippling is an all-in-one HR platform that combines payroll, benefits administration, performance management, and employee onboarding. Its customizable and scalable features make it suitable for businesses of all sizes.

Workday: Workday is a cloud-based HR solution that provides a wide range of features, including recruiting, talent management, payroll, and benefits administration. Workday is designed for large enterprises and can handle complex HR processes.

Zenefits: Zenefits is an all-in-one HR platform that focuses on benefits administration, payroll, and time tracking. With its intuitive interface and wide range of features, Zenefits is a popular choice for small to medium-sized businesses.

Gusto: Gusto is an HR platform specifically designed for small businesses, offering payroll, benefits administration, and compliance features. Its user-friendly interface and affordable pricing make it an attractive option for startups and growing businesses.

ADP: ADP is a well-known HR software provider that offers a range of solutions for businesses of all sizes. Their products include payroll, time and attendance, talent management, and benefits administration. ADP is known for its comprehensive features and strong customer support.

Section 12.5: Getting Started with Your Chosen Human Resources Software

Once you have selected the right HR software for your business, follow these steps to get started:

Sign up and create an account: Register for an account with your chosen HR software provider and provide the required company and personal information.

Customize the software: Set up the software according to your specific HR needs, such as customizing the recruitment process, adding company policies, and configuring performance review templates.

Import employee data: Transfer your existing employee data into the new HR system, either manually or by using an import tool provided by the software.

Train your team: Ensure that your HR team and other relevant employees are trained on how to use the new software effectively. Many providers offer training resources, such as video tutorials, webinars, or onsite training.

Implement the software into your workflow: Integrate the new HR software into your daily processes, such as recruitment, onboarding, and payroll. Ensure that your team follows the new procedures and uses the software consistently.

Monitor and evaluate the software's performance: Regularly review the software's performance and make any necessary adjustments to optimize its effectiveness for your business.

By understanding the various types of HR software available and selecting the right solution for your business, you can streamline your HR processes, improve efficiency, and better manage your employees.

AFFILIATE MANAGEMENT SOFTWARE

In this chapter, we will explore affiliate management software, what they are, factors to consider when choosing one for your business, and provide overviews of popular options like Impact.com, Tapfiliate, PartnerStack, Post Affiliate Pro, and FirstPromoter. Additionally, we'll guide you through the process of getting started with your chosen affiliate management software.

Section 13.1: What is Affiliate Management Software?

Affiliate management software is a digital solution that helps businesses manage their affiliate marketing programs. It automates various tasks, such as tracking affiliate performance, calculating commissions, generating reports, and managing payouts. By using affiliate management software, businesses can efficiently scale their affiliate programs, improve transparency, and enhance relationships with affiliates.

Section 13.2: Factors to Consider When Choosing Affiliate Management Software

When selecting affiliate management software for your business, consider the following factors:

Features: Evaluate the features offered by each platform, such as tracking capabilities, commission structures, promotional tools, and reporting options. Choose a solution that meets your specific requirements.

Integration: Make sure the affiliate management software can integrate with your existing systems, such as your eCommerce platform, CRM, or payment gateway, for seamless data sharing and streamlined workflows.

Pricing: Consider the pricing structure of the software, including any monthly fees, transaction fees, or setup costs. Choose a solution that fits within your budget while providing the features you need.

Scalability: Ensure the software can accommodate your business's growth, supporting additional affiliates and increased traffic as your program expands.

Support: Assess the level of customer support provided by the software vendor, including the availability of live chat, phone support, and online resources. Opt for a solution with responsive and reliable support to help you navigate any issues that may arise.

Section 13.3: Overviews of Popular Affiliate Management Software

Impact.com: Impact.com is a comprehensive affiliate management platform that offers features like real-time tracking, flexible commission structures, and in-depth reporting. Its robust API allows for seamless integration with your existing systems. Impact.com is suitable for businesses of all sizes looking for a scalable and customizable solution.

Tapfiliate: Tapfiliate is a user-friendly affiliate management software that provides features such as click tracking, conversion tracking, and automated commission payouts. It supports integration with popular eCommerce platforms and offers a wide range of promotional tools for affiliates. Tapfiliate is an excellent choice for small to medium-sized businesses.

PartnerStack: PartnerStack is an all-in-one affiliate and partner management platform designed to help businesses build, manage, and scale their partner programs. It offers features like automated commission tracking, in-depth reporting, and customizable partner portals. PartnerStack is suitable for businesses looking for a comprehensive and scalable solution.

Post Affiliate Pro: Post Affiliate Pro is a powerful affiliate management software that offers real-time tracking, customizable commission structures, and advanced reporting options. With its robust integration options, Post Affiliate Pro can easily integrate with your existing systems. This software is ideal for businesses of all sizes seeking a reliable and feature-rich solution.

FirstPromoter: FirstPromoter is an affiliate and referral management platform designed for SaaS and subscription-based businesses. It provides features such as campaign management, automated commission tracking, and integration with popular payment gateways. FirstPromoter is suitable for businesses looking for a specialized solution tailored to their unique requirements.

Section 13.4: Getting Started with Your New Affiliate Management Software

Once you have chosen the right affiliate management software for your business, follow these steps to get started:

Sign up and create an account: Register for an account with your chosen software provider and provide the necessary company and personal information.

Configure the software: Set up the software according to your specific affiliate program requirements, such as defining commission structures, setting up tracking codes, and creating promotional materials.

Integrate the software with your existing systems: Connect your affiliate management software to your eCommerce platform, CRM, or payment gateway to enable seamless data sharing and automate various processes.

Create affiliate resources: Develop promotional materials, such as banners, text links, and email templates, that your affiliates can use to promote your products or services.

Onboard affiliates: Recruit new affiliates or invite your existing partners to join your affiliate program. Provide them with the necessary resources, such as training materials and promotional tools, to help them succeed.

Monitor and optimize your affiliate program: Regularly review your program's performance and make any necessary adjustments to improve its effectiveness. Communicate with your affiliates, providing feedback and support to help them achieve better results.

Manage payouts: Ensure that your affiliates are paid accurately and on time. Most affiliate management software automates this process, but it's essential to verify that commission calculations are correct and address any discrepancies.

By carefully selecting the right affiliate management software for your business and following these steps to get started, you can create a successful affiliate program that drives revenue and helps grow your business.

APPOINTMENT BOOKING SOFTWARE

In this chapter, we will explore appointment booking systems, why they are useful for business owners, how to choose the right one for you, and provide overviews of popular options such as Calendly, Acuity, Book Like a Boss, SimplyBook.me, and Setmore. Additionally, we'll discuss the process of getting started with your chosen appointment booking system.

Section 14.1: Why Appointment Booking Systems are Useful for Business Owners

Appointment booking systems offer numerous benefits for businesses, including:

Time savings: By automating appointment scheduling, business owners can save valuable time that would otherwise be spent on manual scheduling tasks such as phone calls, emails, or text messages.

Improved efficiency: Online appointment booking systems streamline the booking process, reducing the risk of double bookings, missed appointments, or scheduling conflicts.

Enhanced customer experience: With an appointment booking system, clients can schedule appointments at their convenience, view available time slots, and even reschedule or cancel appointments with ease.

Increased revenue: Appointment booking systems can help businesses optimize their schedules, reduce no-shows, and increase overall appointment bookings, leading to increased revenue.

Centralized management: Appointment booking systems provide a centralized platform for managing appointments, client information, and staff schedules, making it easy to stay organized and informed.

Section 14.2: Choosing the Right Appointment Booking System for Your Business

When selecting an appointment booking system, consider the following factors:

Features: Assess the features offered by each platform, such as calendar integrations, payment processing, reminder notifications, and customization options. Choose a solution that meets your specific requirements.

Integrations: Ensure the appointment booking system can integrate with your existing tools, such as CRM systems, email marketing platforms, or payment gateways, to streamline workflows and data sharing.

Ease of use: Opt for a user-friendly solution that both you and your clients can navigate with ease.

Pricing: Consider the pricing structure of the software, including any monthly fees, transaction fees, or setup costs. Choose a solution that fits within your budget while providing the features you need.

Scalability: Make sure the appointment booking system can accommodate your business's growth, supporting additional staff members and increased appointment volume as needed.

Section 14.3: Overviews of Popular Appointment Booking Systems

Calendly: Calendly is a user-friendly appointment scheduling tool that integrates with popular calendar services and offers features such as customizable scheduling pages, automatic time zone detection, and reminder notifications. Calendly is suitable for businesses of all sizes and industries.

Acuity: Acuity is a powerful appointment scheduling platform that provides features like real-time availability, automated appointment reminders, and payment processing. Acuity also offers robust customization options, making it an excellent choice for businesses seeking a tailored solution.

Book Like a Boss: Book Like a Boss is an all-in-one booking platform that combines appointment scheduling, payment processing, and digital product sales. With its user-friendly interface and customizable booking pages, Book Like a Boss is ideal for entrepreneurs and small business owners.

SimplyBook.me: SimplyBook.me is a comprehensive appointment booking system that offers features such as calendar management, client management, and customizable booking widgets. It also supports integrations with popular CRM systems and payment gateways, making it a flexible option for businesses of all sizes.

Setmore: Setmore is an intuitive appointment scheduling platform that provides features like calendar syncing, automated reminders, and staff scheduling. Setmore also offers a free tier, making it an attractive option for businesses on a budget.

Section 14.4: Getting Started with Your Chosen Appointment Booking System

Once you've selected the ideal appointment booking system for your business, follow these steps to get started:

Sign up and create your account: Register for an account on your chosen appointment booking platform. This typically involves providing basic information, such as your name, email address, and business name.

Customize your booking page: Tailor your booking page to match your brand, including logos, colors, and images. Add descriptions of the services you offer and set your available hours.

Configure your settings: Adjust your settings to reflect your preferences, such as the duration of appointments, buffer times between appointments, and cancellation policies.

Integrate your calendar: Connect your appointment booking system to your preferred calendar application (such as Google Calendar or Outlook) to ensure seamless synchronization of appointments and availability.

Set up payment processing: If your appointment booking system offers payment processing, connect it to your preferred payment gateway (such as Stripe, PayPal, or Square) and configure your pricing and invoicing settings.

Add staff members: If you have a team, add staff members to your appointment booking system and configure their individual schedules, services, and booking settings.

Embed the booking widget or share your booking link: Embed your booking widget on your website or share your booking link via email, social media, or other marketing channels to encourage clients to schedule appointments.

Train your team: Ensure that your staff members are familiar with the features and functions of the appointment booking system and can effectively manage their schedules.

Monitor and adjust: Regularly review your appointment booking system's performance and make any necessary adjustments to optimize its effectiveness.

By selecting the right appointment booking system for your business and following these steps, you can streamline your scheduling processes, save time, and enhance the overall client experience.

FILE SHARING

In this chapter, we will explore file sharing software, why it's important for businesses, and provide detailed overviews of popular options such as Google Drive and Dropbox. We'll also discuss how to get started with the chosen file sharing platform.

Section 15.1: The Importance of File Sharing Software for Businesses

File sharing software has become an essential tool for businesses of all sizes. These platforms offer several benefits, including:

Enhanced collaboration: File sharing software enables team members to access, share, and collaborate on documents, spreadsheets, presentations, and other files in real-time, regardless of their location.

Improved efficiency: File sharing platforms streamline workflows by allowing team members to quickly locate and access the files they need, reducing the time spent searching for documents.

Increased security: Secure file sharing solutions protect sensitive data through encryption, access controls, and other security features, reducing the risk of data breaches.

Centralized storage: File sharing software provides a centralized location for storing and organizing files, making it easy for team members to find the information they need.

Scalability: Cloud-based file sharing solutions can easily be scaled up or down to accommodate a business's changing needs, making them a flexible option for growing organizations.

Section 15.2: Google Drive and Dropbox: Detailed Overviews

Google Drive: Google Drive is a cloud-based file storage and synchronization service that offers a seamless integration with other Google products such as Google Docs, Google Sheets, and Google Slides.

Key features of Google Drive include:

- Real-time collaboration and editing

- Accessible from any device with an internet connection
- File version history and the ability to revert to previous versions
- Advanced search functionality
- Integration with third-party applications
- Varied pricing plans, including a free tier with 15 GB of storage
- Dropbox: Dropbox is a popular file sharing and storage platform that allows users to store, access, and share files across devices. Key features of Dropbox include:
- Easy file sharing through links or invitations
- Cross-platform compatibility
- File version history and the ability to restore deleted files
- Integration with third-party applications, such as Microsoft Office and Adobe Creative Cloud
- Enhanced security features, including encryption and two-factor authentication
- Varied pricing plans, including a free tier with 2 GB of storage

Section 15.3: Getting Started with Your Chosen File Sharing Platform

Once you've selected a file sharing platform that meets your business's needs, follow these steps to get started:

Sign up and create your account: Register for an account on your chosen file sharing platform. This typically involves providing basic information, such as your name, email address, and business name.

Familiarize yourself with the interface: Explore the platform's interface to understand how to upload, organize, and manage files, as well as how to adjust settings and preferences.

Upload and organize your files: Begin uploading your files to the platform and organize them using folders or other categorization methods provided by the service.

Set up sharing permissions: Configure sharing permissions for your files and folders, specifying who can access, edit, or comment on them.

Integrate with other applications: If your chosen platform supports integration with other applications, connect it to the tools you use regularly to streamline workflows and improve efficiency.

Train your team: Ensure that your team members are familiar with the features and functions of the file sharing platform and can effectively use it to collaborate and share files.

Monitor usage and adjust as needed: Regularly review your file sharing platform's usage and make any necessary adjustments to optimize its effectiveness and security.

By choosing the right file sharing software for your business and following these steps, you can improve collaboration, increase efficiency, and ensure the security of your files and data.

Section 15.4: Tips for Successful File Management

To get the most out of your chosen file sharing platform, consider implementing the following best practices:

Develop a clear file naming and organization system: Establish a consistent naming convention for files and folders, and create a logical folder structure to make it easy for team members to locate the information they need.

Set access permissions carefully: Ensure that only the necessary individuals have access to sensitive files and folders, and regularly review and update access permissions to maintain security.

Use version control features: Take advantage of the file version history provided by your file sharing platform to track changes and revert to previous versions when necessary.

Encourage team collaboration: Promote the use of real-time collaboration and commenting features within your file sharing platform to streamline communication and improve teamwork.

Regularly back up your files: To protect your data from accidental deletion or corruption, regularly back up your files stored on the file sharing platform.

Keep your file sharing platform up-to-date: Ensure that you are using the latest version of your chosen file sharing software and that all security updates have been installed.

By implementing these best practices, you can maximize the benefits of your chosen file sharing platform and enhance collaboration, productivity, and security within your business.

In conclusion, file sharing software is a crucial tool for businesses in today's digital landscape. By understanding the importance of file sharing platforms, comparing popular options such as Google Drive and Dropbox, and following the steps to get started with your chosen software, you can improve collaboration, increase efficiency, and safeguard your data. By implementing best practices and staying up-to-date with the latest features and security updates, you can ensure that your business continues to thrive in the digital age.

Bonus: File Conversion Tools

Tinywow.com
Convertio.co

COMMUNICATION TOOLS

In this chapter, we will delve into communication software, why it's crucial for businesses, and provide detailed overviews of popular options such as Slack, Microsoft Teams, and Discord. We'll also discuss how to get started with your chosen communication platform.

Section 16.1: The Importance of Communication Software for Businesses

Effective communication is a cornerstone of any successful business. Communication software is designed to streamline and improve collaboration among team members, fostering a more productive and efficient work environment. The benefits of using communication software include:

Enhanced collaboration: Communication software enables team members to easily share ideas, discuss projects, and make decisions, regardless of their location.

Time and cost savings: By reducing the need for in-person meetings and long email threads, communication software can save time and reduce costs.

Better organization: Communication platforms often offer features such as channels, threads, and search functions, allowing teams to stay organized and easily find past conversations.

Integration with other tools: Many communication platforms can be integrated with other productivity tools, such as file sharing, project management, and CRM systems, further streamlining workflows.

Customization and scalability: Communication software can be customized to meet the specific needs of your business and can easily be scaled up or down as your team grows.

Section 16.2: Slack, Microsoft Teams, and Discord: Detailed Overviews

Slack: Slack is a popular communication platform designed to help teams collaborate more effectively.

Key features of Slack include:

- Channels for organizing conversations by topic, project, or team
- Direct messaging for one-on-one communication
- Integration with numerous third-party applications, such as Google Drive, Trello, and Salesforce
- Customizable notifications and preferences
- Audio and video calling capabilities
- Varied pricing plans, including a free tier with limited features
- Microsoft Teams: Microsoft Teams is a communication and collaboration platform that is part of the Microsoft 365 suite. Key features of Microsoft Teams include:
- Channels for organizing conversations and files
- Direct messaging for one-on-one communication
- Integration with other Microsoft 365 applications, such as Word, Excel, and PowerPoint
- Audio and video calling, including screen sharing and conference calling
- Customizable notifications and preferences
- Varied pricing plans, including a free tier with limited features

Discord: Discord is a communication platform initially designed for gamers but has since evolved to serve a variety of communities and businesses.

Key features of Discord include:

- Channels for organizing conversations by topic, project, or team
- Direct messaging for one-on-one communication
- Voice channels for real-time audio communication
- Integration with third-party applications, such as Spotify, YouTube, and Twitch
- Customizable notifications and preferences
- Varied pricing plans, including a free tier with limited features

Section 16.3: Getting Started with Your Chosen Communication Platform

Once you've selected a communication platform that meets your business's needs, follow these steps to get started:

Sign up and create your account: Register for an account on your chosen communication platform. This typically involves providing basic information, such as your name, email address, and business name.

Familiarize yourself with the interface: Explore the platform's interface to understand how to create channels, send messages, adjust settings, and manage notifications.

Set up channels: Create channels for specific topics, projects, or teams to help organize conversations and facilitate collaboration.

Invite team members: Invite your team members to join the platform and encourage them to set up their profiles and preferences.

Establish guidelines and best practices: Develop guidelines for using the communication platform, such as when to use direct messaging versus channels, and how to manage notifications. Share these guidelines with your team to ensure consistent and effective communication.

Integrate with other tools: If your chosen communication platform supports integrations, connect it with other productivity tools your team uses, such as file-sharing, project management, or CRM systems, to streamline workflows.

Train your team: Offer training sessions, resources, and support to help your team members become comfortable with the new communication platform. Encourage them to ask questions and provide feedback.

Monitor and adjust: Regularly assess the effectiveness of your communication platform and make any necessary adjustments to improve collaboration and productivity. Be open to feedback from your team and consider implementing new features or integrations as needed.

Section 16.4: Tips for Successful Communication with Your Team

To maximize the benefits of your chosen communication platform, consider implementing the following best practices:

Encourage open communication: Foster a culture of open communication, where team members feel comfortable sharing ideas, asking questions, and providing feedback.

Set clear expectations: Clearly communicate expectations regarding response times, availability, and the appropriate use of different communication channels.

Be mindful of time zones: If your team is distributed across different time zones, be considerate of each team member's working hours and schedule meetings and deadlines accordingly.

Maintain a balance between synchronous and asynchronous communication: While real-time communication can be valuable, it's essential to strike a balance between synchronous (e.g., video calls) and asynchronous (e.g., messaging) communication methods to allow team members to work efficiently and manage their time effectively.

Regularly review and update guidelines: As your team grows and evolves, revisit your communication guidelines and best practices to ensure they remain relevant and effective.

In conclusion, communication software is a crucial tool for businesses looking to improve collaboration, productivity, and efficiency. By understanding the importance of communication platforms, comparing popular options such as Slack, Microsoft Teams, and Discord, and following the steps to get started with your chosen software, you can create a more connected and successful team. Implementing best practices and being open to feedback will help you continually improve your team's communication and foster a positive work environment.

CUSTOMER SUPPORT SOFTWARE

Section 17.1: Introduction to Customer Support Software

Customer support is a critical aspect of any business, as it directly impacts customer satisfaction, loyalty, and retention. Investing in the right customer support software can streamline your support operations, enhance customer interactions, and ultimately contribute to the success of your business. In this chapter, we'll explore the world of customer support software, discuss how to choose the right one for your business, and provide overviews of popular options, including ZenDesk, Zoho Desk, Intercom, Halo CRM, Salesforce Service Cloud, and Freshdesk.

Section 17.2: Choosing the Right Customer Support Software

Before diving into the various options available, consider these key factors to help you choose the right customer support software for your business:

Business size and needs: Different software options cater to different business sizes and needs. Some are designed for small businesses or startups, while others are tailored for larger enterprises. Analyze your current customer support needs and requirements to determine the best fit.

Scalability: As your business grows, your customer support needs will likely evolve. Choose a software that can scale with your business and offer additional features, capabilities, or integrations as needed.

Integration with existing systems: Your customer support software should integrate seamlessly with your existing systems and tools, such as your CRM, email, and project management software. This will streamline your workflows and ensure a consistent customer experience.

Customization and flexibility: The ability to customize your support software to align with your brand, workflows, and processes is essential. Look for software that offers flexibility in terms of customization and configuration options.

Cost: Consider your budget and the pricing structure of each software option. Some may offer per-user pricing, while others might charge based on the number of support agents or the volume of customer interactions.

Ease of use: User-friendly software is essential for efficient customer support operations. Your support team should be able to learn and use the software quickly and easily.

Section 17.3: Overviews of Popular Customer Support Software

ZenDesk: ZenDesk is a popular customer support software that offers a suite of tools for managing customer interactions across various channels, such as email, live chat, and social media. Key features include ticketing, knowledge base management, and reporting and analytics. ZenDesk is known for its ease of use and extensive customization options.

Zoho Desk: Zoho Desk is a comprehensive customer support software that integrates seamlessly with other Zoho products, such as Zoho CRM and Zoho Projects. It offers features such as ticket management, multi-channel support, reporting and analytics, and a knowledge base. Zoho Desk is ideal for small to medium-sized businesses looking for an affordable, user-friendly solution.

Intercom: Intercom is a customer messaging platform that combines support, sales, and marketing functionalities. It offers a range of features, including live chat, in-app messaging, email support, and knowledge base management. Intercom is known for its powerful automation capabilities and is ideal for businesses looking to streamline their customer communication and support processes.

Halo CRM: Halo CRM is a customer support software that focuses on providing a personalized customer experience. It offers ticketing, live chat, email support, social media integration, and reporting and analytics. Halo CRM's strength lies in its CRM integration, which helps support agents access customer information and history quickly, allowing them to provide more personalized support.

Salesforce Service Cloud: Salesforce Service Cloud is a comprehensive customer support solution that integrates with the broader Salesforce ecosystem. It offers features such as case management, live chat, social media support, knowledge base, and reporting and analytics. Salesforce Service Cloud is designed for businesses of all sizes and is known for its robust functionality, scalability, and seamless integration with other Salesforce products.

Freshdesk: Freshdesk is a user-friendly customer support software that offers multi-channel support, ticketing, knowledge base management, and automation features. It is ideal for small to medium-sized businesses looking for an affordable solution with a range of customization options. Freshdesk's intuitive interface and comprehensive feature set make it a popular choice among businesses seeking to streamline their customer support operations.

Section 17.4: Getting Started with Your New Customer Support Software

Once you've chosen the customer support software that best fits your business needs, follow these steps to get started:

Sign up and set up: Sign up for the chosen software and configure the basic settings, such as company information, support channels, and integrations with your existing systems and tools.

Customize your support environment: Customize your support portal, ticket forms, and automated responses to reflect your brand and workflows. This may include creating custom fields, setting up automated rules, and configuring support categories.

Create a knowledge base: Develop a knowledge base to help customers find answers to common questions and issues. This may include creating help articles, FAQs, and how-to guides. Ensure your knowledge base is easy to navigate and search.

Train your support team: Provide training and resources to your support team to ensure they are familiar with the software and its features. This may include sharing documentation, conducting training sessions, or offering hands-on practice with the software.

Monitor and optimize: Once your support system is in place, monitor its performance and gather feedback from both customers and support agents. Use this feedback to identify areas for improvement and optimization, and make adjustments as needed.

By following these steps, you can effectively implement a customer support software system that streamlines your support operations and enhances the customer experience. Remember to continually evaluate and optimize your support processes to ensure your business remains agile and responsive to customer needs.

VIDEO CONFERENCING

Section 18.1: Introduction to Video Conferencing Software

Video conferencing software allows individuals and teams to communicate virtually via video and audio calls, enabling collaboration, communication, and knowledge-sharing from anywhere in the world. As remote work becomes more common, video conferencing software is a must-have tool for businesses of all sizes.

Section 18.2: Overview of Popular Video Conferencing Software

Zoom: Zoom is a widely-used video conferencing tool that offers high-quality video and audio, screen-sharing capabilities, and various collaboration features. Its user-friendly interface and compatibility with various devices make it a popular choice for businesses of all sizes.

Google Meet: Google Meet, formerly known as Google Hangouts, is a video conferencing solution that comes with Google Workspace. It offers easy integration with other Google applications, making it a convenient choice for organizations using Google Workspace.

Skype: Skype is a well-known video conferencing software that provides free video and voice calls, instant messaging, and screen-sharing. It is available across multiple platforms, including desktop and mobile devices, making it accessible for users worldwide.

Stream Yard: Stream Yard is a video conferencing tool designed for live streaming and recording, offering features such as overlays, banners, and custom branding. It's ideal for businesses looking to create professional-looking live streams, webinars, or presentations.

GoToMeeting: GoToMeeting is a reliable video conferencing platform with HD video quality, screen sharing, and robust scheduling features. It is well-suited for businesses seeking a comprehensive solution for remote meetings, webinars, and presentations.

Section 18.3: Getting Started with Video Conferencing Software

To ensure a smooth experience when using video conferencing software for the first time, follow these steps:

Choose the right software: Evaluate the features, pricing, and compatibility of each video conferencing tool mentioned above to select the one that best fits your needs.

Sign up and download: Sign up for an account and download the necessary software or app, if applicable. Some video conferencing platforms, like Google Meet, can be accessed directly through your browser without downloading an app.

Familiarize yourself with the interface: Spend some time exploring the user interface and learning the basic features, such as starting and joining meetings, muting and unmuting audio, turning video on and off, and using the chat function.

Test your equipment: Before participating in a video call, test your webcam, microphone, and speakers to ensure they are functioning properly. Adjust your camera angle and lighting to make sure you are visible and well-lit during the call.

Practice good video call etiquette: To avoid looking unprofessional or silly, follow basic video call etiquette, such as dressing appropriately, minimizing background noise, and being mindful of body language.

Schedule a test meeting: Before hosting or participating in an important video call, schedule a test meeting with a colleague or friend to ensure everything is working correctly and to gain confidence using the software.

By following these steps, you can confidently use video conferencing software to communicate and collaborate effectively with your team, clients, and partners, regardless of your physical location.

E-SIGNATURES

Electronic signature services enable individuals and businesses to sign, send, and manage legally binding documents digitally, eliminating the need for physical paperwork. These services have gained popularity due to their efficiency, security, and convenience. In this chapter, we will discuss the importance of electronic signature services and how to get started with them.

Section 19.2: Overview of Popular Electronic Signature Services

PandaDoc: PandaDoc is a versatile electronic signature solution that offers document creation, collaboration, and signing functionalities. It is suitable for businesses of all sizes and integrates with various CRM and payment systems. PandaDoc also provides a wide range of templates for various industries.

HelloSign: HelloSign is an easy-to-use electronic signature platform that enables users to securely sign and send documents. It offers a clean interface, integration with popular applications like Google Drive and Dropbox, and legally compliant e-signatures.

DocuSign: DocuSign is a widely-used electronic signature service known for its robust security and compliance features. It offers a wide range of tools for document management, tracking, and signing, making it suitable for businesses across various industries.

Ignition (Formerly known as Practice Ignition): Ignition is an electronic signature and proposal management platform. It streamlines the process of creating, sending, and signing proposals and engagement letters, and also includes automated billing features.

Adobe Sign: Adobe Sign is a trusted electronic signature solution from Adobe, offering seamless integration with other Adobe products and Microsoft applications. It supports a wide range of document formats and provides advanced security features to ensure the integrity of signed documents.

Section 19.3: Getting Started with Electronic Signature Services

To start using electronic signature services, follow these steps:

Evaluate your needs: Consider your business's size, industry, and specific requirements to determine the most suitable electronic signature service.

Compare the services: Compare the features, pricing, and compatibility of the electronic signature services mentioned above to make an informed decision.

Sign up for an account: Once you've selected an electronic signature service, sign up for an account. Most services offer a free trial, allowing you to test the platform before committing to a paid plan.

Familiarize yourself with the platform: Learn how to upload documents, add signature fields, and send documents for signing. Explore additional features, such as templates, document tracking, and integrations, to maximize the benefits of your chosen service.

Set up your signature: Create your electronic signature, either by drawing, typing, or uploading an image. Ensure your signature is clear and legible.

Send your first document: Upload a document, add the necessary signature fields, and send it to the designated recipient(s). Monitor the progress of the signing process using the platform's tracking features.

Manage signed documents: Store signed documents securely on the platform or download them for local storage. Many electronic signature services offer advanced document management features, such as version control, access permissions, and audit trails.

By following these steps, you can efficiently adopt electronic signature services and streamline your document signing processes, saving time and resources while enhancing security and compliance.

INVOICING SYSTEMS

Section 20.1: Introduction to Invoicing Software

Invoicing software streamlines the process of creating, sending, and managing invoices, making it easier for businesses to bill clients, track payments, and maintain accurate financial records. In this chapter, we will discuss the importance of invoicing software, how to choose the right one for your business, and provide overviews of popular invoicing systems.

Section 20.2: Overview of Popular Invoicing Software

Wave Apps: Wave Apps is a free invoicing and accounting solution designed for small businesses and freelancers. It offers easy-to-use invoice creation, expense tracking, and basic financial reporting features. It also supports multiple currencies and integrates with popular payment gateways like Stripe and PayPal.

FreshBooks: FreshBooks is a user-friendly invoicing and accounting software with a wide range of features, including customizable invoices, time tracking, expense tracking, and project management. It offers integration with various third-party applications and supports multiple currencies, making it suitable for businesses of all sizes.

Invoice Ninja: Invoice Ninja is a powerful, open-source invoicing platform that offers a free plan with basic features and paid plans with advanced functionalities. It supports customizable invoice templates, multiple currencies, and integration with popular payment gateways. It also provides time tracking and project management features.

QuickBooks: QuickBooks is a comprehensive accounting software that includes robust invoicing features. It caters to businesses of all sizes and offers a wide range of features, including customizable invoices, automatic payment reminders, and seamless integration with other QuickBooks tools, such as inventory management and payroll.

Bill.com: Bill.com is a cloud-based invoicing and payment management platform that automates the accounts payable and receivable processes. It offers customizable invoice templates, approval workflows, and integration with popular accounting software, such as QuickBooks and Xero.

Section 20.3: Choosing the Right Invoicing Software

To choose the right invoicing software for your business, consider the following factors:

Size of your business: Some invoicing software is better suited for small businesses or freelancers, while others cater to larger organizations with more complex invoicing needs.

Features: Determine the features you need, such as customizable templates, expense tracking, time tracking, or project management, and choose software that offers those functionalities.

Integration: Ensure the invoicing software integrates with your existing accounting software, payment gateways, and other third-party applications you use.

Pricing: Compare the pricing of various invoicing software options, taking into account the features and scalability offered by each.

Ease of use: Choose a user-friendly invoicing software that simplifies the invoicing process and minimizes the learning curve for you and your team.

Section 20.4: Getting Started with Your New Invoicing System

Sign up for an account: Choose the invoicing software that best meets your needs and sign up for an account, taking advantage of any free trials or introductory offers.

Customize your settings: Configure your business information, invoice templates, and payment gateway integrations. Set up your tax rates, currencies, and any other necessary settings.

Import your clients: Import your existing client information or manually add clients to the invoicing software.

Create and send your first invoice: Generate a new invoice, add the necessary line items, and send it to your client. Monitor the status of your invoices and send reminders or follow-ups as needed.

Track your expenses: Utilize expense tracking features, if available, to monitor and categorize your business expenses.

Analyze financial reports: Use the invoicing software's reporting features to gain insights into your financial performance and make informed business decisions.

Train your team: If you have a team, make sure they are familiar with the invoicing software and understand how to use it effectively. Offer training sessions or provide access to tutorials and resources to help them get up to speed.

Automate processes: Explore automation features within the invoicing software, such as recurring invoices, automatic payment reminders, and approval workflows, to streamline your billing process and save time.

Optimize your invoicing system: Regularly review your invoicing process to identify areas for improvement and make any necessary adjustments. This may include updating templates, refining your follow-up strategy, or integrating additional third-party applications.

Seek customer feedback: Ask your clients for feedback on your invoicing process and make any necessary adjustments to ensure it is user-friendly and efficient for both parties.

By following these steps, you can successfully implement an invoicing software that simplifies your billing process, helps you maintain accurate financial records, and ultimately improves the overall efficiency of your business.

PAYMENT PROCESSORS

21.1 Introduction

In this chapter, we will discuss payment processors, what they are, and how to select the right one for your business in great detail. We will provide overviews of various payment processors, including Stripe, PayPal, Stax, Payment Depot, Merchant One, and Chase for Business, as well as a few high-risk merchant account options like Durango Merchant Services, Payment Cloud, SMB Global, and Host Merchant Services.

21.2 What are Payment Processors?

Payment processors are companies that facilitate transactions between your customers and your business. They handle the transfer of funds, provide secure connections, and ensure that payments are properly authorized and completed. Choosing the right payment processor is essential for smooth, secure transactions and a seamless customer experience.

21.3 Selecting the Right Payment Processor for Your Business

When selecting a payment processor, consider factors such as fees, compatibility with your existing systems, ease of use, customer support, and the types of payments accepted (such as credit cards, digital wallets, or cryptocurrencies). Also, be sure to check if the processor supports your target market, as some payment processors may have restrictions on certain industries or countries.

21.4 Overview of Payment Processors

21.4.1 Stripe
Stripe is a popular payment processor known for its developer-friendly API and easy integration with various platforms. It supports multiple payment methods, including credit cards, digital wallets, and cryptocurrencies. Stripe offers competitive transaction fees and is known for its robust security measures.

21.4.2 PayPal
PayPal is a widely-used payment processor that offers a variety of services, including online payments, invoicing, and digital wallets. While it is easy to set up and use, it is essential to navigate away from PayPal quickly due to higher transaction fees and potential account limitations.

21.4.3 Stax

Stax is a subscription-based payment processor that offers a comprehensive suite of tools for businesses, including invoicing, recurring billing, and reporting. Its pricing model may be attractive for businesses with high transaction volumes, as it charges a flat monthly fee rather than a per-transaction fee.

21.4.4 Payment Depot

Payment Depot offers a wholesale pricing model for payment processing, which may result in lower fees for businesses with high transaction volumes. They provide 24/7 customer support and compatibility with various point-of-sale systems and e-commerce platforms.

21.4.5 Merchant One

Merchant One is a full-service payment processor that offers a range of services, including credit card processing, e-commerce solutions, and point-of-sale systems. They provide competitive rates and 24/7 customer support.

21.4.6 Chase for Business

Chase for Business is a payment processing solution provided by the financial institution JPMorgan Chase. They offer competitive rates, fraud protection, and integration with various platforms, including e-commerce and point-of-sale systems.

21.5 High-Risk Merchant Account Providers

21.5.1 Durango Merchant Services
Durango Merchant Services specializes in high-risk merchant accounts and offers customized solutions for businesses in industries considered high-risk. They provide competitive rates, fraud protection, and dedicated account managers.

21.5.2 Payment Cloud
Payment Cloud is another high-risk merchant account provider that focuses on helping businesses in industries with higher risk profiles. They offer tailored solutions, competitive rates, and chargeback management services.

21.5.3 SMB Global
SMB Global provides high-risk merchant account solutions for businesses in various industries. They offer customizable payment processing solutions, competitive rates, and fraud prevention tools.

21.5.4 Host Merchant Services
Host Merchant Services is a payment processor that offers high-risk merchant account services. They provide personalized solutions, competitive rates, and 24/7 customer support.

21.6 Final Thoughts

When selecting a payment processor, it's crucial to thoroughly evaluate each option and consider the specific needs of your business. Keep in mind factors such as transaction fees, compatibility with your existing systems, customer support, and the types of payments accepted. If your business falls into a high-risk category, be sure to explore high-risk merchant account providers that specialize in serving your industry.

In conclusion, choosing the right payment processor is essential for smooth transactions and a seamless customer experience. By considering the options outlined in this chapter and evaluating each provider's offerings, you can find the best fit for your business and ensure a secure and efficient payment processing system.

COURSE BUILDERS/LMS

Introduction

Online courses have become increasingly popular as a means for businesses to educate their customers, train employees, and generate additional revenue streams. A Learning Management System (LMS) or course builder is a software platform that allows you to create, manage, and deliver your online courses effectively. In this chapter, we'll discuss the various types of course builders and LMS platforms available, how to choose the right one for your business, and how to get started with your chosen platform.

Different Uses of Course Builders/LMS

- Course builders and LMS platforms can be used for various purposes, including:
-
- Employee training and onboarding
- Professional development and certification
- Customer education and product tutorials
- Generating additional revenue through paid courses

When selecting a course builder or LMS platform, consider the following factors:

- Ease of use and customization options
- Integrations with existing tools and systems
- Pricing and scalability
- Content delivery and engagement features
- Reporting and analytics capabilities

Kajabi

Kajabi is an all-in-one platform that offers course creation, marketing, and sales tools. It is ideal for businesses looking to create and sell online courses while also managing their marketing efforts.

Thinkific

Thinkific is a user-friendly platform that allows you to create, market, and sell online courses with ease. It offers a wide range of customization options and integrations with popular tools.

Teachable

Teachable is a course creation platform that focuses on simplicity and ease of use. It offers a variety of features to help you create engaging and visually appealing courses.

Udemy

Udemy is a massive online course marketplace that allows you to host and sell your courses to a broad audience. It's a great option for businesses looking to reach a wide audience quickly but comes with some limitations in terms of course customization and pricing control.

LearnDash

LearnDash is a powerful WordPress plugin that turns your website into a fully functional LMS. It offers advanced features like gamification, quizzes, and certificates, making it ideal for businesses with more complex course requirements.

MemberPress

MemberPress is a WordPress membership plugin that integrates with LearnDash to create a complete course and membership solution. It allows you to protect and sell access to your courses and other premium content.

Basic Members Area Functions in Web Builders

Some web builders offer basic members area functions that could work for simple use cases. However, if you want to create a successful and engaging online course, it's worth exploring dedicated course builders and LMS platforms.

Getting Started with Your Chosen Course Builder/LMS

Once you have selected the right platform for your business, follow these steps to get started:

1. Sign up for the platform and familiarize yourself with its interface and features
2. Outline and structure your course content
3. Create engaging multimedia content like videos, quizzes, and interactive elements
4. Set up pricing and payment options
5. Integrate your course builder with your existing tools and systems
6. Launch your course and promote it to your target audience

By considering the various course builder and LMS options and following these steps, you can create an engaging and successful online course for your business.

SEO TOOLS

Introduction

Search Engine Optimization (SEO) is essential for businesses to improve their online visibility, drive organic traffic, and increase sales. In this chapter, we'll cover the basics of SEO, the various tools available to business owners, and how to choose the right ones for your needs. We'll also provide overviews of popular SEO tools, including Yoast, Yext, Google My Business, Ahrefs, Semrush, Google Search Console, Google Analytics, Moz, and Surfer SEO.

SEO Basics

SEO involves optimizing your website and content to rank higher on search engine results pages (SERPs) for relevant keywords. Key elements of SEO include:

Keyword research: Identifying the right keywords to target based on search volume and competition

On-page optimization: Optimizing individual web pages to rank higher, including meta tags, header tags, and content quality

Off-page optimization: Building high-quality backlinks and managing your online reputation
Technical SEO: Ensuring your website is easily crawlable, loads quickly, and is mobile-friendly

What SEO Tools Do
SEO tools help businesses streamline their SEO efforts, track performance, and gain insights to improve their rankings. They can assist with:

- Keyword research and analysis
- Backlink analysis and monitoring
- Competitor analysis
- On-page and technical SEO audits
- Rank tracking
- Content optimization
- Analytics and reporting

When selecting an SEO tool, consider the following factors:

- Features and functionalities
- Ease of use and learning curve
- Integration with your existing tools and systems
- Pricing and scalability
- Customer support and resources

Overview of Popular SEO Tools

Yoast
Yoast is a popular WordPress plugin that helps optimize your content for search engines. It provides real-time feedback on your content's SEO, readability, and keyword usage.

Yext
Yext is a local SEO and reputation management tool that helps businesses manage their online presence across various platforms, including Google My Business, Yelp, and social media.

Google My Business
Google My Business is a free tool that allows businesses to manage their online presence on Google, including their appearance in search results and Google Maps.

Ahrefs
Ahrefs is a comprehensive SEO tool that offers keyword research, backlink analysis, competitor analysis, rank tracking, and content optimization features.

Semrush
Semrush is an all-in-one marketing toolkit that provides SEO, PPC, and content marketing tools to help

businesses improve their online visibility and drive more traffic.

Google Search Console

Google Search Console is a free tool from Google that helps businesses monitor and maintain their website's presence in Google search results. It provides valuable insights on website performance, indexing, and crawling issues.

Google Analytics

Google Analytics is a free web analytics tool that helps businesses understand their website traffic, user behavior, and conversions. It provides valuable insights to improve your SEO and overall online performance.

Moz

Moz offers a suite of SEO tools that help businesses improve their search engine rankings, including keyword research, link building, and on-page optimization features.

Surfer SEO

Surfer SEO is a content optimization tool that helps you create SEO-friendly content by analyzing the top-ranking pages for your target keywords and providing data-driven recommendations.

YouTube SEO Tools

Vid IQ:

Vid IQ is a suite of video analytics tools designed to help content creators grow their YouTube channel. It offers features such as keyword research, competitor analysis, and video optimization tips to help creators improve their content and attract more views and subscribers. Vid IQ also includes tools to help with video management and promotion, such as bulk video editing and tag management. With its data-driven insights and user-friendly interface, Vid IQ is a valuable tool for any YouTube creator looking to boost their channel's performance.

Tube Buddy:

Tube Buddy is a YouTube optimization and management tool that offers a wide range of features to help creators grow their channel. It includes features such as keyword research, tag suggestions, and video optimization tips, as well as analytics tools to help creators track their performance and identify areas for improvement. Tube Buddy also offers video management tools, such as bulk editing and thumbnail customization, and promotional tools, such as the ability to run contests and giveaways. With its comprehensive suite of features, Tube Buddy is a popular tool for

YouTube creators looking to streamline their workflow and improve their channel's performance.

Once you've chosen the right SEO tools for your business, follow these steps to get started:

1. Sign up for the tools and familiarize yourself with their interfaces and features
2. Conduct keyword research to identify target keywords for your content
3. Analyze your website's current SEO performance
4. Optimize your website's on-page elements, including meta tags, header tags, and content quality
5. Improve your site's technical SEO, such as site speed, mobile-friendliness, and crawlability
6. Develop a link-building strategy to build high-quality backlinks
7. Monitor your website's rankings and performance using rank tracking and analytics tools
8. Continuously analyze your competitors to identify areas of improvement and new opportunities
9. Optimize your content using content optimization tools like Surfer SEO

10. Integrate your chosen SEO tools with other platforms (such as your content management system or CRM) for seamless data sharing and analysis
11. Keep up-to-date with the latest SEO trends, algorithm updates, and best practices to stay ahead of the competition

Final Thoughts

Implementing SEO tools can greatly improve your online visibility and drive more organic traffic to your website. By selecting the right tools for your needs and using them effectively, you can boost your search engine rankings and achieve long-term success. Remember that SEO is an ongoing process, and it's essential to continuously optimize your website and content to stay ahead of your competitors.

VPN SOFTWARE

Introduction to VPN Tools

Virtual Private Networks (VPNs) are essential tools for businesses of all sizes. They enable users to access the internet securely and privately, which is particularly important when dealing with sensitive information or working remotely. VPNs encrypt your data and route your connection through a secure server, ensuring that your online activities are safe from prying eyes. In this chapter, we will discuss how business owners can use VPN tools, factors to consider when choosing a VPN, and tips for using VPNs effectively.

Benefits of VPN Tools for Business Owners

- Enhanced security: VPNs protect your data by encrypting it, making it difficult for hackers or other malicious actors to access your sensitive information.
- Privacy protection: VPNs hide your IP address and location, ensuring that your online activities remain private and anonymous.
- Remote access: VPNs allow employees to securely access your company's network and resources from anywhere in the world.
- Bypassing geo-restrictions: VPNs enable you to access content that may be restricted in certain

regions, allowing you to stay informed and access essential resources regardless of your location.

- Improved network performance: Some VPNs offer features such as compression and optimized routing, which can help improve the speed and performance of your internet connection.

Factors to Consider When Choosing a VPN

Security: Ensure that the VPN uses strong encryption and secure protocols to protect your data.

Speed: Choose a VPN with fast server connections to minimize latency and maintain a high-quality browsing experience.

Number of servers and locations: Select a VPN with a large number of servers across various locations, providing more options for connecting to different regions.

Ease of use: Look for a VPN with an intuitive interface and easy-to-use features, especially if your employees are not tech-savvy.

Compatibility: Ensure the VPN supports all the devices and operating systems used within your organization.

Customer support: Choose a VPN provider with responsive and helpful customer support to assist you with any issues that may arise.

Pricing: Consider the cost of the VPN service and whether it fits within your budget.

Overview of Popular VPN Tools

ExpressVPN: Known for its high speed, strong security features, and user-friendly interface. It offers a vast network of servers across multiple locations.

NordVPN: Offers robust security features, a large server network, and good speeds. It also has a user-friendly interface and strong customer support.

Surfshark: A budget-friendly option that offers strong security features, fast speeds, and a simple interface. It also allows unlimited simultaneous connections.

Windscribe: Offers a free plan with limited data, as well as affordable paid plans with a good range of features and server locations.

ProtonVPN: Developed by the team behind ProtonMail, it focuses on privacy and security, offering a no-logs policy and strong encryption.

CyberGhost: Offers a large server network, strong security features, and a user-friendly interface, making it suitable for beginners.

IPVanish: Known for its fast speeds, strong security features, and compatibility with a wide range of devices.

Tips for Using VPN Effectively
- Always connect to the VPN before accessing sensitive information or logging into company accounts.
- Encourage employees to use the VPN when working remotely or using public Wi-Fi networks.
- Regularly update your VPN software to ensure you're using the latest security features and improvements.
- Experiment with different server locations to find the best balance between speed and security.

- Utilize the VPN's customer support if you encounter any issues or have questions about the service.

Final Thoughts

Investing in a VPN tool is crucial for ensuring the security and privacy of your business's online activities. By carefully considering the various factors and options discussed in this chapter, you can select the right VPN for your organization's needs. Once you have chosen a VPN, make sure to educate your employees on its proper use and benefits. By implementing a VPN effectively, you can significantly enhance the security of your business's online activities and protect sensitive information from potential threats.

PASSWORD MANAGERS

Introduction to Password Managers

In the digital age, businesses need to manage countless passwords for various accounts and platforms. As cyber threats continue to evolve, it's crucial to ensure that your business has a strong, organized, and secure approach to password management. Password managers can help by storing, generating, and organizing your passwords in an encrypted vault, making it easier for you and your team to access and manage these digital keys.

Why Password Managers are Essential for Businesses

Enhanced Security: Password managers generate strong, unique passwords for each account, reducing the risk of cyberattacks due to weak or reused passwords.

Organized Access: Centralized storage of passwords makes it easier for team members to access the information they need without compromising security.

Time Savings: Employees no longer need to spend time trying to remember or recover passwords, improving productivity.

Secure Sharing: Some password managers allow you to share passwords securely with team members, ensuring they have access to the necessary information while maintaining control over sensitive data.

When selecting a password manager for your business, consider the following factors:

Security: Ensure that the password manager uses strong encryption and offers features like two-factor authentication.

Pricing: Compare the pricing plans and consider if they fit your business needs and budget.

User Experience: Choose a password manager that is user-friendly and easy to navigate, so employees are more likely to use it.

Compatibility: Check if the password manager is compatible with the devices and platforms your business uses.

Customer Support: Look for a password manager with responsive customer support in case you need assistance.

Overview of Popular Password Managers

NordPass

NordPass is a secure password manager from the creators of NordVPN. It offers strong encryption, two-factor authentication, and a user-friendly interface. NordPass also provides secure password sharing and supports a wide range of devices and platforms.

LastPass

LastPass is a popular password manager with a variety of features, including password generation, secure sharing, and emergency access. LastPass offers both free and paid plans, making it a flexible option for businesses of all sizes.

Dashlane

Dashlane is another well-known password manager that offers additional security features, such as dark web monitoring and VPN protection. Dashlane also provides secure password sharing and has a user-friendly interface.

Bitwarden

Bitwarden is an open-source password manager that prioritizes security and transparency. It offers end-to-end encryption and a variety of features, including password sharing and two-factor authentication. Bitwarden has free and paid plans to accommodate various business needs.

1Password

1Password is a highly secure password manager that focuses on simplicity and ease of use. With features like password sharing, two-factor authentication, and a user-friendly interface, 1Password is a popular choice for many businesses.

Once you have selected a password manager that meets your business needs, follow these steps to get started:

- Sign up for an account and choose a pricing plan that suits your business.
- Install the password manager on your devices and platforms.
- Import your existing passwords and organize them into categories or folders.
- Start using the password manager to generate strong, unique passwords for your accounts.
- Train your employees on using the password manager and emphasize its importance in maintaining security.

By implementing a password manager, you can significantly enhance the security of your business's online accounts and streamline the password management process. Invest the time to choose the right password manager and train your employees to create a more secure digital environment for your business.

LEGAL ON A BUDGET

Introduction to Legal Services Subscriptions
For businesses, having access to legal support is crucial for handling various aspects such as contracts, intellectual property, employment issues, and compliance. Legal services subscriptions provide businesses with affordable and accessible legal assistance, helping them navigate the complexities of the law and mitigate risks.

Importance of Legal Services Subscriptions for Businesses

Cost-effective: Subscription-based legal services often cost less than hiring a full-time in-house attorney or retaining a law firm.

Access to Expertise: Legal service providers have a network of experienced attorneys specializing in various fields, ensuring that businesses have access to the right expertise when needed.

Flexibility: Subscription services often offer various plans and tiers, allowing businesses to choose the level of support that fits their needs and budget.

Ongoing Support: Subscriptions ensure that businesses have continuous access to legal support, making it easier to address legal issues proactively.

Factors to Consider When Choosing a Legal Services Subscription

Range of Services: Consider the types of legal services your business requires and ensure that the subscription covers those needs.

Pricing: Compare the pricing plans and select a service that offers the best value for your business.

Reputation: Look for providers with positive reviews and a track record of helping businesses like yours.

Customer Support: Choose a provider with responsive customer support in case you need assistance or have questions about their services.

Overview of Legal Services Subscription Providers

Rocket Lawyer

Rocket Lawyer offers a range of legal services, including document creation, attorney consultations, and business formation services. Their subscription plans provide access to legal documents, attorney consultations, and discounts on additional services.

LegalZoom

LegalZoom is known for its business formation services but also offers legal plans for ongoing support. Subscribers can access attorney consultations, document review, and discounted services like trademark registration and contract drafting.

LegalShield

LegalShield provides small businesses with access to a network of attorneys for a flat monthly fee. Their plans cover services such as legal consultations, contract review, debt collection assistance, and more.

Avvo

Avvo is an online legal marketplace where businesses can find and hire attorneys for various legal needs. While not a subscription service, Avvo offers a platform for businesses to access legal support on a case-by-case basis.

FindLaw

FindLaw is a legal information website that provides businesses with access to a wealth of free resources, including articles, guides, and legal forms. While not a subscription service, FindLaw is a valuable resource for businesses seeking legal information and guidance.

FileNow

FileNow specializes in business formation services and offers ongoing compliance support for businesses. Their subscription plans provide access to registered agent services, annual report filings, and other compliance-related services.

Northwest Registered Agent

Northwest Registered Agent is known for its registered agent services but also offers business formation and ongoing compliance support. They provide personalized customer support and have a reputation for their attention to detail and commitment to client privacy.

Once you've selected a legal services subscription that meets your business needs, follow these steps to get started:

- Sign up for an account and choose the appropriate plan for your business.
- Familiarize yourself with the provider's platform and available resources.
- Schedule a consultation with an attorney, if needed, to discuss any pressing legal concerns.
- Utilize the provider's services for document creation, review, and other legal needs as they arise.

By investing in a legal services subscription, businesses can access affordable and reliable legal support, helping them protect their interests and mitigate risks. Carefully consider the options available and choose a provider that best aligns with your business needs to ensure a strong foundation for success.

Integrating Legal Services Subscription with Your Business Operations
To make the most out of your chosen legal services subscription, consider the following steps for seamless integration with your business operations:

Identify Key Legal Needs: Determine the areas where your business will need legal support, such as contracts, compliance, employment issues, and intellectual property protection.

Communicate with Your Team: Ensure that relevant team members are aware of the available legal resources and how to access them. This will encourage a proactive approach to addressing legal issues.

Establish a Process: Develop a standardized process for handling legal matters, such as when to consult an attorney or escalate an issue. This will help your team manage legal concerns effectively and efficiently.

Regularly Review and Update: Regularly review your legal needs and make any necessary adjustments to your subscription plan or services. Stay informed about legal updates and changes that may impact your business.

Conclusion

Legal services subscriptions offer a cost-effective and convenient solution for businesses seeking legal support. By carefully considering your options and choosing a provider that meets your unique needs, you can effectively protect your business and ensure compliance with relevant laws and regulations.

Integrating legal services into your business operations will empower you and your team to address legal challenges proactively, ultimately contributing to the overall success of your business.

SALES TOOLS

Introduction

Sales tools play a crucial role in the success of a business, particularly when it comes to cold outreach. In this chapter, we will discuss the importance of using sales tools, the laws and regulations you must be aware of when planning cold outreach campaigns, and tips for creating an effective strategy. We will also provide an overview of several popular sales tools, including FlowChat, GoHighLevel, LinkedIn Sales Navigator, hunter.io, and snov.io.

The Importance of Sales Tools in Cold Outreach

Sales tools can significantly improve the efficiency and effectiveness of your cold outreach efforts by:
-
- Automating repetitive tasks, such as sending follow-up emails or tracking leads.
- Providing insights into prospect behavior and preferences, allowing for more targeted and personalized communication.

- Streamlining the sales process by consolidating information and resources in one centralized platform.

Laws and Regulations to Consider for Cold Outreach

When planning a cold outreach campaign, it is essential to comply with all relevant laws and regulations, including:

- CAN-SPAM Act (United States): This law sets requirements for commercial email messages, including providing a clear opt-out mechanism and accurate sender information.
- GDPR (European Union): The General Data Protection Regulation requires businesses to obtain explicit consent from EU residents before sending them marketing communications.
- CASL (Canada): Canada's Anti-Spam Legislation requires businesses to obtain consent from recipients before sending commercial electronic messages.

Ensure that your cold outreach campaigns comply with these regulations to avoid fines and maintain a positive brand reputation.

Tips for Planning an Effective Cold Outreach Campaign

Research Your Target Audience: Understand the needs, challenges, and preferences of your target audience to craft more effective and engaging outreach messages.

Personalize Your Messaging: Use personalization techniques, such as addressing recipients by name or referencing their company or industry, to make your outreach more relevant and engaging.

Test and Optimize: Regularly test different outreach strategies and messaging, analyze the results, and refine your approach based on data-driven insights.

Be Persistent but Respectful: Follow up with prospects multiple times, but respect their time and preferences. Give them the option to opt-out or decline further communication.

Sales Tools Overview

FlowChat: FlowChat is a messaging automation platform that helps businesses engage with leads and prospects through personalized conversations. It enables users to create custom chat flows, track prospect interactions, and manage leads in one platform.

GoHighLevel: GoHighLevel is an all-in-one sales and marketing platform designed for agencies and small businesses. It offers a range of tools, including CRM, sales automation, and email marketing, to streamline your sales process and improve outreach effectiveness.

LinkedIn Sales Navigator: This powerful tool from LinkedIn helps sales professionals find and engage with prospects on the platform. It provides advanced search features, lead recommendations, and insights into prospect behavior, making it easier to connect with the right people.

hunter.io: Hunter.io is an email discovery tool that helps you find and verify professional email addresses. It can be particularly useful for cold outreach campaigns, as it allows you to target specific individuals within an organization.

snov.io: Snov.io is a multi-functional sales and marketing tool that offers email finding, email verification, and email sending capabilities. It helps businesses automate and streamline their outreach efforts by providing accurate contact information and tools for creating personalized email campaigns.

Conclusion

Sales tools can greatly enhance your cold outreach efforts by automating tasks, providing insights, and streamlining processes. By staying compliant with relevant laws and regulations and carefully planning your outreach strategy, you can improve the effectiveness of your campaigns and drive better results. Consider using tools like FlowChat, GoHighLevel, LinkedIn Sales Navigator, hunter.io, and snov.io to optimize your cold outreach campaigns and connect with the right prospects for your business. Remember to research your target audience, personalize your messaging, test and optimize your strategies, and be persistent but respectful in your approach. By leveraging these tools and techniques, you can successfully grow your business and achieve your sales objectives.

CONCLUSION

In conclusion, my fellow business superheroes, it's time to take charge and forge your very own utility belt. Think of yourself as the entrepreneurial Batman, navigating the cityscape of your industry, ready to take on any challenge that comes your way. Your mission, should you choose to accept it, is to research the software mentioned in this book, select the ones that best suit your unique needs, and build a formidable arsenal of business tools.

Picture this: It's a dark and stormy night, a few years from now. You've just cracked a massive deal and saved your city from the sinister clutches of your fiercest business rival. As you revel in your victory, a familiar figure swoops down from the shadows. It's none other than Batman himself!

"Great job, partner!" he exclaims, offering a hearty handshake. "Together, we've taken down the villainous forces that threatened our city, and we've done it in style."

You share a victorious fist bump with the Dark Knight, knowing that it's your meticulously crafted utility belt that made all the difference. The tools and resources you've gathered over time have made you an unstoppable force, ready to tackle any challenge that comes your way.

So, what are you waiting for? It's time to embark on your epic journey to becoming the business superhero you've always dreamt of being. Dive into the world of software, explore the countless options available, and build a utility belt that would make Batman green with envy. With the right set of tools, you'll be well-equipped to conquer the business world and forge a legacy that even Gotham's finest would be proud of.

Now, go forth and crush some villains, dear reader. The future of your business depends on it!

NOTES

NOTES

NOTES